THE INNER LIFE

TO ACCOMPANY THE STUDY BOOK
THE INNER LIFE

BY HARVEY H. POTTHOFF

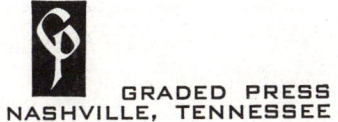

GRADED PRESS
NASHVILLE, TENNESSEE

THE INNER LIFE

A book of selected readings

Copyright © 1969 by Graded Press

All rights reserved

A publication of the United Methodist Church prepared by the General Board of Education through the Division of Curriculum Resources and published by Graded Press, the curriculum publishing department of The Methodist Publishing House, 201 Eighth Avenue, South, Nashville, Tennessee 37203. Printed in the United States of America.

☐ Henry M. Bullock is editor of church school publications, Division of Curriculum Resources, Methodist Board of Education. ☐ Horace R. Weaver is editor of adult publications. ☐ Harold. L. Fair is editor of Foundation Studies in Christian Faith of which *The Inner Life* is the seventh part. ☐ Donald C. Viets is editor of this book of selected readings.

Acknowledgments

The following credits acknowledge our gratitude to the publishers and writers who have allowed us to use their materials in this anthology.

[1] From *Kagawa*, by William Axling (New York: Harper & Brothers Publishers). Copyright, 1932, by Harper & Brothers. Used by permission of Harper & Row, Publishers, Inc. Pages 152-53.
[2] From *You're Something Else, Charlie Brown*, by Charles M. Schulz (New York: Holt, Rinehart and Winston). Copyright © 1967 United Feature Syndicate, Inc. Used by permission of United Feature Syndicate, Inc.
[3] From *I Never Promised You A Rose Garden*, by Hannah Green. Copyright © 1964 by Hannah Green. Reprinted by permission of Holt, Rinehart and Winston, Inc. Page 208.
[4] From *Kagawa*, by William Axling (New York: Harper & Brothers Publishers). Copyright, 1932, by Harper & Brothers. Used by permission of Harper & Row, Publishers, Inc. Pages 136-37.

[5] From "Evangelical Prayer," by Louis Lochet, in *Contemporary Spirituality, Current Problems in Religious Life*, edited by Robert W. Gleason, S. J. (New York: The Macmillan Company). Copyright © 1968 by The Macmillan Company. Used by permission. Page 172.
[6] From *He Sent Leanness, A Book of Prayers for the Natural Man*, by David Head (New York: The Macmillan Company). Copyright © The Epworth Press 1959. Used by permission of The Macmillan Company. Pages 21-22.
[7] From *Man's Search for Meaning, An Introduction to Logotherapy, a Newly Revised and Enlarged Edition of From Death-Camp to Existentialism*, by Viktor E. Frankl, translated by Ilse Lasch (Boston: Beacon Press). Reprinted by permission of Beacon Press, copyright © 1959, 1962 by Viktor Frankl. Pages 35-37.
[8] From "Paraphrase on Psalm 8," by Leslie F. Brandt. Reprinted from *This Day* magazine by permission of Concordia Publishing House, St. Louis, Missouri.
[9] From *The Heart of Man, Its Genius for Good and Evil*, by Erich Fromm (New York: Harper & Row). Copyright © 1964 by Erich Fromm. Used by permission of Harper & Row, Publishers, Inc. Abridgment of pages 118-19.
[10] From *Man's Search for Meaning, An Introduction to Logotherapy, a Newly Revised and Enlarged Edition of From Death-Camp to Existentialism*, by Viktor E. Frankl, translated by Ilse Lasch (Boston: Beacon Press). Reprinted by permission of Beacon Press, copyright © 1959, 1962 by Viktor Frankl. Pages 76-77.
[11] From *This I Believe, Volume I*, edited by Edward P. Morgan (New York: Simon and Schuster, 1952). Copyright © 1952 by Help, Inc. Used by permission of Simon and Schuster. Pages 17-18.
[12] From *You're Something Else, Charlie Brown*, by Charles M. Schulz (New York: Holt, Rinehart and Winston, Inc.). Copyright © 1967 United Feature Syndicate, Inc. Used by permission of United Feature Syndicate, Inc.
[13] From *The Works of John Wesley, Volume I, Journal from October 14, 1735, to November 29, 1745* (Grand Rapids: Zondervan Publishing House). Used by permission. Pages 103-4.
[14] From *World Aflame*, by Billy Graham. Copyright © 1965 by Billy Graham. Reprinted by permission of Doubleday & Company, Inc. Page 155.
[15] From *Turning To God, A Study of Conversion in the Book of Acts and Today*, by William Barclay (London: The Epworth Press). Copyright © The Epworth Press, 1963. Used by permission. Pages 94-95.
[16] From *What Luther Says, An Anthology*, Volume I, compiled by Ewald M. Plass (Saint Louis: Concordia Publishing House). Copyright 1959 by Concordia Publishing House. Used by permission. Pages 466-82.
[17] From *The Dilemma of Modern Belief*, by Samuel H. Miller (New York: Harper & Row, Publishers). Copyright © 1963 by Samuel H. Miller. Used by permission of Harper & Row, Publishers, Inc. Page 78.
[18] From *God Is for Real, Man*, by Carl F. Burke (New York: Association Press). Copyright © 1966 by National Board of Young Men's Christian Associations. Used by permission of Association Press. Pages 95-96.
[19] From *The Renewal of Hope*, by Howard Clark Kee (New York: Association Press). Copyright © 1959 by National Board of Young Men's Christian Associations. Used by permission of Association Press. Pages 170-71.
[20] From *Man's Search for Meaning, An Introduction to Logotherapy, a Newly Revised and Enlarged Edition of From Death-Camp to Existentialism*, by Viktor E. Frankl, translated by Ilse Lasch (Boston: Beacon Press). Reprinted by permission of Beacon Press, copyright © 1959, 1962 by Viktor Frankl. Pages 72-74.
[21] From *Do You Hear Me, God?*, by Ruth and Arthayer Sanborn (Valley Forge: The Judson Press). Copyright © 1968 The Judson Press. Used by permission. Pages 79-80.
[22] From *Life Together*, by Dietrich Bonhoeffer, translated, and with an introduction by John W. Doberstein (New York: Harper & Brothers Publishers) Copyright, 1954, by Harper & Brothers. Used by permission of Harper & Row, Publishers, Inc. Pages 35-36.
[23] From *Faith To Act*, by Jack Boozer and William A. Beardslee. Copyright © 1967 by Abingdon Press. Used by permission. Pages 155-56.
[24] From *Time* Magazine, May 14, 1965. Copyright © 1965 Time, Inc.; New York. Used by permission of Time, Inc. Page 111.
[25] From *Psychotherapy and a Christian View of Man*, by David E. Roberts (New York: Charles Scribner's Sons. Copyright, 1950, by Charles Scribner's Sons. All quotations from David E. Roberts are fully protected by United States and International Copyright. Used by permission of Charles Scribner's Sons. Pages 6-7.

[26] From *Psychotherapy and a Christian View of Man,* by David E. Roberts (New York: Charles Scribner's Sons). Copyright, 1959, by Charles Scribner's Sons. All quotations from the works of David E. Roberts are fully protected by United States and International Copyright. Used by permission of Charles Scribner's Sons. Pages 46-47.

[27] From *The New York Times,* June 9, 1968. Copyright © 1968 by The New York Times Company. Reprinted by permission. Page 56.

[28] From *The Meaning of Persons,* by Paul Tournier, translated by Edwin Hudson (New York: Harper & Row, Publishers). Copyright © 1957 by Paul Tournier. Used by permission of Harper & Row, Publishers, Inc. Pages 92-93.

[29] From *The Heart of Man, Its Genius for Good and Evil,* by Erich Fromm (New York: Harper & Row, Publishers). Copyright © 1964 by Erich Fromm. Used by permission of Harper & Row, Publishers, Inc. Pages 129-30.

[30] From *Psychotherapy and a Christian View of Man,* by David E. Roberts (New York: Charles Scribner's Sons). Copyright, 1950, by Charles Scribner's Sons. All quotations from the works of David E. Roberts are fully protected by United States and International Copyright. Used by permission of Charles Scribner's Sons. Page 80.

[31] From *The Varieties of Religious Experience, A Study in Human Nature,* by William James (New York: The Modern Library). Copyright, 1902, by William James. Used by permission of David McKay Company, Inc. Pages 46-48.

[32] From *The Shaking of the Foundations,* by Paul Tillich (New York: Charles Scribner's Sons, 1948). Copyright, 1948, by Charles Scribner's Sons. All quotations from the works of Paul Tillich are fully protected by United States and International Copyright. Used by permission of Charles Scribner's Sons. Pages 98-99.

[33] From *The Life We Prize,* by Elton Trueblood (New York: Harper & Brothers Publishers). Copyright, 1951, by Harper & Brothers. Used by permission of Harper & Row, Publishers, Inc. Pages 200-01.

[34] From *What's Left To Believe?,* by J. Schoneberg Setzer. Abingdon Press. Copyright © 1968 by Abingdon Press. Used by permission. Page 63.

[35] From *The Martin Luther Christmas Book,* translated and arranged by Roland H. Bainton. Muhlenberg Press. Copyright, 1948, by W. L. Jenkins. Used by permission. Page 38.

[36] By Clarence Tucker Craig in *The Interpreter's Bible,* Vol. 10. Abingdon Press. Used by permission. Page 46.

[37] From *Between Parent and Child, New Solutions to Old Problems,* by Dr. Haim G. Ginott (New York: The Macmillan Company). Copyright © Dr. Haim G. Ginott, 1965. Used by permission of The Macmillan Company. Pages 68-70.

[38] From "The People of the Underground Church" by Layton P. Zimmer from *The Underground Church* edited by Malcolm Boyd © Sheed and Ward Inc., 1968. Page 15.

[39] From *The Grass Roots Church* by Stephen C. Rose. Copyright © 1966 by Stephen C. Rose. Reprinted by permission of Holt, Rinehart and Winston, Inc. Pages 97-98.

[40] From "The Church and Civil Rights" by James E. Groppi from *The Underground Church,* edited by Malcolm Boyd © Sheed and Ward, Inc., 1968. Page 74.

[41] From *A Book of Everyday Prayers,* by William Barclay (New York: Harper & Row, Publishers). Copyright © 1959 by William Barclay. Used by permission of Harper & Row, Publishers, Inc. Page 104.

[42] By Kim Malthe-Bruun, in *Dying We Live, The Last Messages of Men and Women Who Resisted Hitler and Were Martyred,* edited by Gollwitzer, Kuhn, Schneider, translated by Reinhard C. Kuhn (New York: The Seabury Press). Copyright © 1956 by Pantheon Books, Inc. Used by permission of Random House, Inc., Publishers. Pages 77-85.

[43] Al Ross, in the *Saturday Review,* December 31, 1966. Copyright 1966 Saturday Review, Inc. Used by permission.

[44] From *The Quest of the Historical Jesus, A Critical Study of Its Progress from Reimarus to Wrede,* by Albert Schweitzer (London: Adam and Charles Black, 1910). Used by permission of The Macmillan Company. Pages 399-401.

[45] From *Strength to Love,* by Martin Luther King, Jr. (New York: Harper & Row, Publishers). Copyright © 1963 by Martin Luther King, Jr. Used by permission of Harper & Row, Publishers, Inc. Pages 49-50.

[46] Percy Dearmer (1867-1936), after John Bunyan (1628-88). Words from *The English Hymnal* by permission of the Oxford University Press.

[47] From *The Varieties of Religious Experience, A Study in Human Nature,* by William James (New York: The Modern Library). Copyright, 1902, by William James. Used by permission of David McKay Company, Inc. Pages 476-478.

[48] From *Verse, The Carpentered Hen and Other Tame Creatures, Telephone Poles and Other Poems,* by John Updike (Greenwich: Fawcett Publications). Copyright © 1963 by John Updike. Used by permission of Fawcett Publications. Page 115.
[49] From *Inscape* by Ross Snyder. Copyright © 1968 by Abingdon Press. Used by permission. Pages 29-30.
[50] From *Contemporary Prayers for Public Worship,* edited by Caryl Micklem (Grand Rapids: William B. Eerdmans Publishing Company). Copyright © 1967 by SCM Press Ltd., London WC 1, England. Used by permission of Wm B. Eerdmans Publishing Co. Pages 46-47.
[51] From *The Letters to the Corinthians,* translated by William Barclay. Published in the U.S.A. by The Westminster Press, 1957. Used by permission. Pages 95-96.
[52] Marya Mannes, "Time, Gentlemen, Please." Copyright © 1962 by The Reporter Magazine Company. Used by permission.
[53] From "The Meaning of Political Murder," by Charles Frankel, in *Saturday Review,* LI, June 22, 1968. Copyright 1968 Saturday Review, Inc. Used by permission. Page 18.
[54] From "Anything for a Laugh," by Arthur Knight, in *Saturday Review,* LI, July 20, 1968. Copyright 1968 Saturday Review, Inc. Used by permission. Page 38.
[55] By Robert R. Wicks in *The Interpreter's Bible,* Vol. XI. Abingdon Press. Used by permission. Pages 118-19.
[56] From *Experience and God,* by John E. Smith (New York: Oxford University Press, 1968). Copyright © 1968 by Oxford University Press, Inc. Used by permission. Pages 63-64.
[57] From *The Letters to the Corinthians,* by William Barclay. Published in the U.S.A. by The Westminster Press, 1957. Used by permission. Pages 94-95.
[58] From "I Want a Principle Within," by Charles Wesley, in *The Methodist Hymnal* (Nashville: The Methodist Publishing House). Copyright © 1964, 1966 by Board of Publication of The Methodist Church, Inc. No. 279.
[59] From *The Orthodox Church,* by Timothy Ware (Baltimore: Penguin Books). Copyright © Timothy Ware, 1963. Used by permission of Penguin Books, Inc. Pages 43-44.
[60] From *The Company of the Committed,* by Elton Trueblood (New York: Harper & Brothers Publishers). Copyright © 1961 by David Elton Trueblood. Used by permission of Harper & Row, Publishers, Inc. Page 23.
[61] From *Wheels in the Air,* by William T. Joyner (Philadelphia: Pilgrim Press). Copyright © 1968 by United Church Press. Used by permission. Page 55.
[62] From *The Living of These Days, an Autobiography,* by Harry Emerson Fosdick (New York: Harper & Brothers Publishers). Copyright © 1956 by Harper & Brothers. Used by permission of Harper & Row, Publishers, Inc. Pages 73-75.
[63] From *Faith for Personal Crises,* by Carl Michalson (New York: Charles Scribner's Sons). © Copyright 1958 by Southwestern University. All quotations from the works of Carl Michalson are fully protected by United States and International Copyright. Used by permission of Charles Scribner's Sons. Pages 67-68.
[64] From *What Was Bugging Ol' Pharaoh?,* by Charles M. Schulz (Anderson, Indiana: Warner Press). Copyright © 1964, by Warner Press, Inc. Used by permission. Page 60.
[65] From *The Christian Agnostic,* by Leslie D. Weatherhead. Abingdon Press. Copyright © 1965 by Leslie D. Weatherhead. Used by permission. Pages 360-61.
[66] From *Two or Three Together, A Manual for Prayer Groups,* by Harold Wiley Freer and Francis B. Hall (New York: Harper & Brothers Publishers). Copyright, 1954, by Harper & Brothers. Used by permission of Harper & Row, Publishers, Inc. Page 144.
[67] From *Two or Three Together, A Manual for Prayer Groups,* by Harold Wiley Freer and Francis B. Hall (New York: Harper & Brothers Publishers). Copyright, 1954, by Harper & Brothers. Used by permission of Harper & Row, Publishers, Inc. Pages 24-26.
[68] From *The Company of the Committed,* by Elton Trueblood (New York: Harper & Brothers Publishers). Copyright © 1961 by David Elton Trueblood. Used by permission of Harper & Row, Publishers, Inc. Page 75.
[69] From *Two or Three Together, A Manual for Prayer Groups,* by Harold Wiley Freer and Francis B. Hall (New York: Harper & Brothers Publishers). Copyright, 1954, by Harper & Brothers. Used by permission of Harper & Row, Publishers, Inc. Pages 152-53.

[70] From *Your Word Is Near, Contemporary Christian Prayers,* by Huub Oosterhuis, translated by N.D. Smith (New York: Newman Press). Copyright © 1968 by The Missionary Society of St. Paul the Apostle in the State of New York. Used by permission of Paulist/Newman Press. Pages 105-6.

[71] From *James Bond's World of Values,* by Lycurgus M. Starkey, Jr. Copyright © 1966 by Abingdon Press. Used by permission. Pages 65-66.

[72] From *Perspectives on 19th and 20th Century Protestant Theology,* by Paul Tillich, edited and with an introduction by Carl E. Braaten (New York: Harper & Row, Publishers). Copyright © 1967 by Hannah Tillich. Used by permission of Harper & Row, Publishers, Inc. Pages 97-98.

[73] From *Perspectives on 19th and 20th Century Protestant Theology,* by Paul Tillich, edited and with an introduction by Carl E. Braaten (New York: Harper & Row, Publishers). Copyright © 1967 by Hannah Tillich. Used by permission of Harper & Row, Publishers, Inc. Pages 104-5.

[74] From *He Sent Leanness, a Book of Prayers for the Natural Man,* by David Head (New York: The Macmillan Company). Copyright © The Epworth Press 1959. Used by permission of The Macmillan Company. Page 36.

[75] From *The Adventure of Living,* by Paul Tournier, translated by Edwin Hudson (New York: Harper & Row, Publishers). Copyright © 1965 by Paul Tournier. Used by permission of Harper & Row, Publishers, Inc. Pages 236-37.

[76] From *Auschwitz Trials, Letters from an Eyewitness,* by Emmi Bonhoeffer, translated by Ursula Stechow (Richmond: John Knox Press). Copyright © M. E. Bratcher 1967. Used by permission of John Knox Press. Pages 47-48.

[77] From *The Meaning of Persons,* by Paul Tournier, translated by Edwin Hudson (New York: Harper & Row, Publishers). Copyright © 1957 by Paul Tournier. Used by permission of Harper & Row, Publishers, Inc. Pages 226-27.

[78] From *The Meaning of Persons,* by Paul Tournier, translated by Edwin Hudson (New York: Harper & Row, Publishers). Copyright © 1957 by Paul Tournier. Used by permission of Harper & Row, Publishers, Inc. Pages 215-16.

[79] From *Faith to Act,* by Jack Boozer and William A. Beardslee. Abingdon Press. Copyright © 1967 by Abingdon Press. Used by permission. Pages 249-50.

[80] From *J. B., A Play in Verse,* by Archibald MacLeish (Boston: Sentry Edition, 1961). Copyright © 1956, 1957, 1958 by Archibald MacLeish. Used by permission of Houghton Mifflin Company. Pages 88-90.

[81] From *Secrets,* by Paul Tournier, translated by Joe Embry (Richmond: John Knox Press). Copyright © M. E. Bratcher 1965. Used by permission of John Knox Press. Pages 60-61.

[82] From *Between Heaven and Earth, Conversations with American Christians,* by Helmut Thielicke, translated and edited by John W. Doberstein (New York: Harper & Row, Publishers). Copyright © 1965 by John W. Doberstein. Used by permission of Harper & Row, Publishers, Inc. Pages 183-84.

[83] From *Look Homeward Angel, A Story of the Buried Life,* by Thomas Wolfe (New York: Charles Scribner's Sons). Copyright © 1929, 1947, 1952 by Charles Scribner's Sons. Quotations from the works of Thomas Wolfe are fully protected by United States and International Copyright. Used by permission of Charles Scribner's Sons. Opposite page 1.

[84] From *Hippies in Our Midst, the Rebellion Beyond Rebellion,* by Delbert L. Earisman (Philadelphia: Fortress Press). Copyright © 1968 by Fortress Press. Used by permission. Pages 143-44.

[85] From *The Transforming Friendship,* by Leslie D. Weatherhead. Abingdon Press. Used by permission. Pages 133-34.

[86] From *The Teaching of Reverence for Life,* by Albert Schweitzer. Translated by Richard and Clara Winston. Copyright © 1965 by Holt, Rinehart and Winston, Inc. Reprinted by permission of Holt, Rinehart and Winston, Inc. Pages 47-48.

[87] From *Of Time and the River, A Legend of Man's Hunger in his Youth,* by Thomas Wolfe (New York: Charles Scribner's Sons). Copyright, 1936, by Charles Scribner's Sons. Quotations from the works of Thomas Wolfe are fully protected by United States and International Copyright. Used by permission of Charles Scribner's Sons. Pages 265-67.

[88] From *Joy, Expanding Human Awareness,* by William C. Schutz (New York: Grove Press, Inc.). Copyright © 1967 by William C. Schutz. Reprinted by permission of Grove Press, Inc. Pages 213-215.

[89] From *The Secular City, Secularization and Urbanization in Theological Perspective, Revised Edition,* by Harvey Cox (New York: The Macmillan Company). Copyright © Harvey Cox 1965, 1966. Used by permission of The Macmillan Company. Pages 39-40.

[90] From *The Miracle of Dialogue*, by Reuel L. Howe (Greenwich: The Seabury Press). Copyright © 1963 by The Seabury Press, Inc. Used by permission. Pages 105-6.
[91] From *Strength To Love*, by Martin Luther King, Jr. (New York: Harper & Row, Publishers). Copyright © 1963 by Martin Luther King, Jr. Used by permission of Harper & Row, Publishers, Inc. Pages 116-17.
[92] Reprinted by permission of The World Publishing Company from *A Journey with the Saints*, by Thomas Kepler. Copyright © 1951 by The World Publishing Co. Pages 10-11.
[93] "For My People," by Margaret Walker. Copyright © 1942 by Yale University Press. Used by permission.
[94] From *Seek a City Saint*, by David Head (New York: The Macmillan Company). Copyright © The Epworth Press 1964. Used by permission of The Macmillan Company. Pages 93-94.
[95] William P. Hoest, in *Saturday Review*, July 2, 1966. Copyright 1966 Saturday Review, Inc. Used by permission. Page 14.
[96] From *The Magnificent Defeat*, by Frederick Buechner (New York: The Seabury Press). Copyright © 1966 by The Seabury Press, Inc. Used by permission. Pages 87-88.
[97] From *I Lie On My Mat and Pray*, edited by Fritz Pawelzik. Friendship Press, New York. Used by permission. Page 13.
[98] From "Prayer," in *Seek a City Saint*, by David Head (New York: The Macmillan Company). Copyright © The Epworth Press 1964. Used by permission of The Macmillan Company. Pages 22-23.
[99] From "Midnight Meditation," in *Stammerer's Tongue, A Book of Prayers for the Infant Christian*, by David Head (New York: The Macmillan Company, 1960). Copyright © The Epworth Press 1960. Used by permission of The Macmillan Company. Pages 53-55.
[100] From *The Meaning of God in Human Experience, A Philosophic Study of Religion*, by William Ernest Hocking (New Haven: Yale University Press). Copyright, 1912 by Yale University Press. Used by permission. Pages 426-27.
[101] From *Pathways of the Inner Life*, edited by Georges A. Barrois, copyright © 1956, by The Bobbs-Merrill Company, Inc., reprinted by permission of the publishers. Page 22.
[102] From *What Men Live By*, by Richard C. Cabot (Boston: Houghton Mifflin Company). Copyright, 1914, by Richard C. Cabot. Used by permission of Houghton Mifflin Co. Page 336.
[103] From *What Men Live By*, by Richard C. Cabot (Boston: Houghton Mifflin Company). Copyright, 1914, by Richard C. Cabot. Used by permission of Houghton Mifflin Co. Pages 276-77.
[104] From *The Secular Congregation*, by Robert A. Raines (New York: Harper & Row, Publishers). Copyright © 1968 by Robert A. Raines. Used by permission of Harper & Row, Publishers, Inc. Pages 120-21.
[105] From *Treat Me Cool, Lord*, by Carl F. Burke (New York: Association Press). Copyright © 1968 by National Board of Young Men's Christian Associations. Used by permission. Page 80.
[106] From *Lift Up Your Hearts*, by Walter Russell Bowie. Copyright © 1939, 1956 by Pierce & Washabaugh (Abingdon Press). Used by permission. Pages 16-17.
[107] From *The Art of Personal Prayer*, by Lance Webb. Abingdon Press. Copyright © 1962 by Abingdon Press. Used by permission. Page 137.
[108] From *Treat Me Cool, Lord*, by Carl F. Burke (New York: Association Press). Copyright © 1968 by National Board of Young Men's Christian Associations. Used by permission. Page 72.
[109] From *The Church Redemptive*, by Howard Grimes. Copyright © 1958 by Abingdon Press. Used by permission. Pages 48-50.
[110] From *New Life in the Church*, by Robert A. Raines (New York: Harper & Brothers Publishers). Copyright © 1961 by Robert Arnold Raines. Used by permission of Harper & Row Publishers, Inc. Pages 70-71.
[111] From *How to Become a Bishop without Being Religious*, by Charles Merrill Smith. Copyright © 1965 by Charles Merrill Smith. Reprinted by permission of Doubleday & Company, Inc. Page 79.
[112] From *On Edge*, by Jim Crane (Richmond: John Knox Press). Copyright © M. E. Bratcher 1965. Used by permission of John Knox Press.
[113] From *The Congregation in Mission*, by George W. Webber. Copyright © 1964 by Abingdon Press. Used by permission. Pages 99-100.

[114] From *The Incendiary Fellowship*, by Elton Trueblood (New York: Harper & Row, Publishers). Copyright © 1967 by David Elton Trueblood. Used by permission of Harper & Row, Publishers, Inc. Pages 46-47.
[115] From *A Hard Look at Adult Christian Education*, by John R. Fry. The Westminster Press. Copyright © 1961, W. L. Jenkins. Used by permission. Pages 95-96.
[116] From *Our Fathers and Us*, by Umphrey Lee (Dallas: Southern Methodist University Press, 1958). Copyright © 1958 by Southern Methodist University Press. Used by permission. Pages 28-30.
[117] From *The Story of Methodism*, by Halford E. Luccock and Paul Hutchinson. Copyright renewal 1954 by Luccock and Hutchinson (Abingdon Press). Used by permission. Pages 168-72.
[118] From "Kitty Hawk" from *In the Clearing* by Robert Frost. Copyright © 1956, 1962 by Robert Frost. Reprinted by permission of Holt, Rinehart and Winston, Inc. Page 7.
[119] From *Theological Ethics*, by James Sellers (New York: The Macmillan Company). Copyright © James Sellers 1966. Used by permission of The Macmillan Company. Page 53.
[120] From *The Strong and the Weak*, by Paul Tournier, translated by Edwin Hudson. Published in the U.S.A. by The Westminster Press, 1963. Used by permission. Pages 239-240.
[121] From *The Art of Loving*, by Erich Fromm, edited by Ruth Nanda Anshen (New York: Harper & Brothers Publishers). Copyright © 1956 by Erich Fromm. Used by permission of Harper & Row, Publishers, Inc. Pages 86-87.
[122] From *A Man for All Seasons, A Play in Two Acts*, by Robert Bolt (New York: Random House). Copyright, 1960, 1962, by Robert Bolt. Used by permission of Random House. Pages 159-60.
[123] From *The Art of Loving*, by Erich Fromm, edited by Ruth Nanda Anshen (New York: Harper & Brothers, Publishers). Copyright © 1956 by Erich Fromm. Used by permission of Harper & Row, Publishers, Inc. Pages 126-128.
[124] From *From the Ashes of Christianity, A Post-Christian View*, by Mary Jean Irion (New York: J. B. Lippincott Company). Copyright © 1968 by Mary Jean Irion. Used by permission of the J. B. Lippincott Company. Pages 186-87.
[125] From *The Strong and the Weak*, by Paul Tournier, translated by Edwin Hudson. Published in the U.S.A. by The Westminster Press, 1963. Used by permission. Page 250.
[126] From *Salute to a Sufferer*, by Leslie D. Weatherhead. Copyright © 1962 by Leslie D. Weatherhead. Published by Abingdon Press. Used by permission. Pages 89-92.
[127] From *God's Word in Today's World*, by Suzanne de Dietrich (Valley Forge: The Judson Press). Copyright © 1967, The Judson Press. Used by permission. Page 110.

Edward L. Moore assisted the editor in preparing this book of selected readings.

CONTENTS

                                                                           Readings

1. THE LIFE WE LIVE WITHIN 1-11
2. CHRISTIAN LIFE AND THE INNER LIFE 12-23
3. THE INNER FREEDOM TO BE ONESELF 24-35
4. HOW AND WHERE FAITH GROWS 36-46
5. A LIFE OF CONTINUING RENEWAL 47-58
6. THE DISCIPLINES OF BELIEVING 59-70
7. OUR FEELINGS AND OUR FAITH 71-82
8. RENEWAL THROUGH RELATIONSHIPS 83-93
9. TOWARD GREATER DEPTH IN THE EXPERIENCE OF PRAYER 94-108
10. INNER TRANSFORMATION THROUGH CHRISTIAN FELLOWSHIP 109-117
11. INNER VICTORIES OF THE SPIRIT 118-127

CHAPTER I—THE LIFE WE LIVE WITHIN

1 · AN INNER LIGHT—KAGAWA

When threatened with total blindness and compelled to lie for months with bandaged eyes in a darkened room, he had hours when the far horizons were hid in mists and his career seemed to have come to an untimely close, yet through it all his far-visioned soul reveled in a light that does not shine on sea or land.

" 'It's inconvenient, isn't it?' 'What?' 'Your blindness.' 'Yes, but it is inconvenient for people not to have wings, isn't it? If, however, they invent airplanes, these take the place of wings.'

"The same is true regarding the external eyes. If they go blind it is simply a matter of inventing internal sight. My God is light itself. Even though every outward thing is shrouded in darkness in the inner chamber of my soul, God's Eternal light shines on.

> Burn! oh, thou inner light, burn!
> Burn on, oh light, fed from the oil
> That never fails.

"God will keep for me that little light forever burning. He himself is my light, and as long as He shines within I do not lament being compelled to sit out the long day in darkness.

"Health is gone! Sight is gone! But as I lie forsaken in this dark room God still gives light. Pains that pierce the very

THE INNER LIFE

fires of Hell itself sweep over me. Yet, even in the melting fires of hell, God's mercy, for which all of earth's manifold treasures would be an utterly inadequate exchange, still enfolds me.

"At the center of things there is a heart. On the yonder side of darkness there is light. Deprived of sight, I discern that light flooding in through the darkness.

"To me all things are vocal. Oh, wonder words of love! The bedding, the tears, the spittle, the perspiration, the vapor of the compress on my eyes, the ceiling, the matted floor, the voice of the chirping sparrow without, all are vocal. God and every inanimate thing speak to me. Thus even in the dark I feel no sense of loneliness."—William Axling, *Kagawa*

2.

—© 1967 United Feature Syndicate

3 • HOPE AMID DIFFICULTY

[Hannah Green's book tells of Deborah, a teen-ager, who lives out her inner civil war as a patient in a mental hospital. Deborah's troubles almost destroy her. Few Christians experience difficulties as severely as Deborah. Even though the pressure in her life is extreme, her faint hope sustains her.]

Her dream began with winter darkness. Out of this darkness came a great hand, fisted. It was a man's hand, powerful and hollowed by shadows in the wells between bones and tendons. The fist opened and in the long plain of the palm lay three small pieces of coal. Slowly the hand closed, causing within the fist a tremendous pressure. The pressure began to generate a white heat and still it increased. There was a sense of weighing, crushing time. She seemed to feel the suffering of the coal with her own body, almost beyond the point of being borne. At last she cried out to the hand, "Stop it! Will you never end it! Even a stone cannot bear to this limit . . . even a stone . . . !"

After what seemed like too long a time for anything molecular to endure, the torments in the fist relaxed. The fist turned slowly and very slowly opened.

Diamonds, three of them.

Three clear and brilliant diamonds, shot with light, lay in the good palm. A deep voice called to her, "Deborah!" and then, gently, "Deborah, this will be you."

—Hannah Green, *I never promised you a rose garden*

4 • GROWTH THROUGH STRUGGLE

"If one lives for a long time immersed in God's grace there stretches across one's inner soul a calm which nothing can destroy. When, guarded by five officers of the law, I was thrown into prison pending trial, when marching with a mob of 15,000 people along a street seething with riot, when threatened with daggers in the hands of desperadoes, the jewel of peace, hidden away in my soul, was in no wise disturbed. When in an automobile crash the city tram rumbled on over me, that inner peace was still maintained. Even when a chronic eye disease threatened to rob me of my sight I experienced no swells on the calm sea of my soul.

"Polished like a mirror, this calm reflects in itself every passing circumstance of life, but its occurrence leaves no turbidity on the surface. Criticism, abuse, ridicule, slander, all these simply serve as polishing powder in the process of further burnishing the mirror-like calm in my heart."

—William Axling, *Kagawa*

5 · ONENESS IN THE INNER AND THE OUTER LIFE

... Beyond any of life's experiences, beyond all interests and desires, beyond the difficult submission to God's Will, beyond tormenting pain, the boredom of work, the suffering of defeats, beyond the experience of pain, sin, suffering, hate, beyond all this—we are still in search of a new simplicity. This peace of mind is above and beyond a full adult life. It is a peace that has given everything to the Father. It is also the filial trust of a child. But this total abandon, this gift of ourselves is also weighted down with the deeds of an entire lifetime. This unity, which rules the soul and which is expressed in prayer before God, is no longer the childlike simplicity of a child who has not yet experienced struggle and who does not realize the full meaning of these words: *I love you above all else.* This regained unity is above and within man's actions and passions, reuniting them in a single effort that will draw everything together in the thrust of his return to the Father.

Between the infantile prayers of the very young, who give everything they touch a remarkable simplicity, because they do not know what they are giving, and the unified prayers of adults giving their all, not only once a day in words, but moment by moment in all their actions, because love has unified their whole life—between these two points, we must strive toward the latter.

It is, in effect, like cutting the apron strings, like growing up to become involved in the world. We must form a strong relationship with all the good around us, with people, with the world. All our interests, pleasures, work, distractions, should bring us closer to God, not push us further away. If it does the latter, our prayers become lost, unprotected, smothered in a world that has thrown away the invitation to God. —Louis Lochet, in *Contemporary Spirituality*

6 · A LITANY

O God, we have considerable doubts in our minds about the way You are running the universe.

Is there any chance that You will show Your mercy to us, O Lord?

We see all kinds of things in the world that do not please us.

Do you think You could do something about it, O God?

The psychologists tell us that our nagging doubts about Your goodness burrow into the subconscious mind and spit poison.

Isn't this a bit unfair, O Lord?

From a universe where things can be extremely unpleasant,
Deliver us, Good Lord.

From everything that calls from us courage and endurance,
Deliver us, Good Lord.

From all ignorance, insecurity, and uncertainty,
Deliver us, Good Lord.

From all personal needs that give the love of others a chance to find expression,
Deliver us, Good Lord.

From suffering the balloon of our pride to be pricked, from suffering the castle of our self-satisfaction to be attacked, from suffering the thunder of our egotism to be stilled,
Deliver us, Good Lord.

From all vicissitudes and deprivations that throw us back upon You,
Deliver us, Good Lord.

We sinners do hope against hope that You will pay just a little attention to our prayers; and that it may please You to get on with Your business, and do the best You can for us;
We beg You on our knees (as far as the pews will allow), O Lord.

That it may please You to bring good to us, and not evil, and that You will be on the side of light rather than darkness;
We beg You on our knees, O Lord.

That it may please You to rule and govern Your holy Church Universal in the right way;
We beg You on our knees, O Lord.
    Hear us, O Lord.
        Be Yourself, O Lord. . . .

—David Head, He Sent Leanness

7 · LIFE IN A CONCENTRATION CAMP

In spite of all the enforced physical and mental primitiveness of the life in a concentration camp, it was possible for spiritual life to deepen. Sensitive people who were used to a rich intellectual life may have suffered much pain (they were often of a delicate constitution), but the damage to their inner selves was less. They were able to retreat from their terrible surroundings to a life of inner riches and spiritual freedom. Only in this way can one explain the apparent paradox that some prisoners of a less hardy make-up often seemed to survive camplife better than did those of a robust nature. In order to make myself clear, I am forced to fall back on personal experience. Let me tell what happened on those early mornings when we had to march to our work site.

There were shouted commands: "Detachment, forward march! Left-2-3-4! Left-2-3-4! Left-2-3-4! Left-2-3-4! First man about, left and left and left and left! Caps off!" These words sound in my ears even now. At the order "Caps off!" we passed the gate of the camp, and searchlights were trained upon us. Whoever did not march smartly got a kick. And worse off was the man who, because of the cold, had pulled his cap back over his ears before permission was given.

We stumbled on in the darkness, over big stones and through large puddles, along the one road leading from the camp. The accompanying guards kept shouting at us and driving us with the butts of their rifles. Anyone with very sore feet supported himself on his neighbor's arm. Hardly a word was spoken; the icy wind did not encourage talk. Hiding his mouth behind his upturned collar, the man marching next to me whispered suddenly: "If our wives could see us now! I do hope they are better off in their camps and don't know what is happening to us."

That brought thoughts of my own wife to mind. And as we stumbled on for miles, slipping on icy spots, supporting each other time and again, dragging one another up and onward, nothing was said, but we both know: each of us was thinking of his wife. Occasionally I looked at the sky, where the stars were fading and the pink light of the morning was beginning to spread behind a dark bank of clouds. But my mind clung to my wife's image, imagining it with an uncanny acuteness. I heard her answering me, saw her smile, her frank and encouraging look. Real or not, her look was then more luminous than the sun which was beginning to rise.

A thought transfixed me: for the first time in my life I saw the truth as it is set into song by so many poets, proclaimed as the final wisdom by so many thinkers. The truth—that love is the ultimate and the highest goal to which man can aspire. Then I grasped the meaning of the greatest secret that human poetry and human thought and belief have to impart: *The salvation of man is through love and in love.* I understood how a man who has nothing left in this world still may know bliss, be it only for a brief moment, in the contemplation of his beloved. In a position of utter desolation, when man cannot express himself in positive action, when his only achievement may consist in enduring his sufferings in the right way—an honorable way—in such a position man can, through loving contemplation of the image he carries of his beloved, achieve fulfillment. For the first time in my life I was able to understand the meaning of the words, "The angels are lost in perpetual contemplation of an infinite glory."

—Viktor E. Frankl, *Man's Search for Meaning*

8 · PARAPHRASE ON PSALM 8

O God,
How full of wonder and splendor You are!

I see the reflections of Your beauty and hear the sounds
of Your majesty wherever I turn.
Even the babbling of babes and the laughter of children
spell out Your name in indefinable syllables.

When I gaze into star-studded skies
And attempt to comprehend its vast distances,
I contemplate in utter amazement my Creator's concern for
me;
I am dumbfounded that You should care personally about me.

And yet You have made me in Your image.
You have called me Your son.
You have ordained me as Your priest,
and chosen me to be Your servant.
You have assigned to me the fantastic responsibility of
carrying on Your creative activity.

O God,
How full of wonder and splendor You are!—Leslie F. Brandt

9 · ON ACHIEVING UNITY

The first answer to the quest to transcend separateness and to achieve unity I call the *regressive* answer. If man wants to find unity, if he wants to be freed from the fright of loneliness and uncertainty, he can try to return to where he came from—to nature, to animal life, or to his ancestors. He can try to do away with that which makes him human and yet tortures him: his reason and self-awareness. It seems that for hundreds of thousands of years man tried just that. . . . The individual who participates in this common folly lacks the sense of complete isolation and separation, and hence escapes the intense anxiety he would experience in a progressive society. It must be remembered that for most people reason and reality are nothing but public consensus. One never "loses one's mind" when nobody else's mind differs from one's own.

The alternative to the regressive, archaic solution to the problem of human existence, to the burden of being man, is the *progressive solution,* that of finding a new harmony not by regression but by the full development of all *human* forces, of the humanity within oneself. The progressive solution was visualized for the first time in a radical form . . . in that remarkable period of human history between 1500 B.C. and 500 B.C. It appeared in Egypt around 1350 B.C. in the teachings of Ikhnaton, with the Hebrews around the same time in the teachings of Moses; around 600 to 500 B.C. the same idea was announced by Lao-Tse in China, by the Buddha in India, by Zarathustra in Persia, and by the philosophers in Greece as well as by the prophets in Israel. The new goal of man, that of becoming fully human and thus regaining his lost harmony was expressed in different concepts and symbols. . . . These concepts were to a large extent determined by the modes of thought, and in the last analysis by the practice of life and the socio-economic-political structure of each of these cultures. But while the particular form in which the new goal was expressed depended on various historical circumstances, the goal was essentially the same: to solve the problem of human existence by giving the right answer to the question which life poses it, that of man's becoming fully human and thus losing the terror of separateness. . . .

Different as the thought concepts of all these new religions and movements are, they have in common the idea of the basic alternative of man. Man can choose only between two possibilities: to regress or to move forward. He can either return to an archaic, pathogenic solution, or he can progress toward, and develop, his humanity. . . .

—Erich Fromm, *The Heart of Man*

10 · TO HAVE A WHY FOR LIVING

[The writer tells of his experiences in a concentration camp.]

Those who know how close the connection is between the state of mind of a man—his courage and hope, or lack of them—and the state of immunity of his body will understand that the sudden loss of hope and courage can have a deadly effect. The ultimate cause of my friend's death was that the expected liberation did not come and he was severely disappointed. This suddenly lowered his body's resistance against the latent typhus infection. His faith in the future and his will to live had become paralyzed and his body fell victim to illness—and thus the voice of his dream was right after all.

The observations of this one case and the conclusion drawn from them are in accordance with something that was drawn to my attention by the chief doctor of our concentration camp. The death rate in the week between Christmas, 1944, and New Year's, 1945, increased in camp beyond all previous experience. In his opinion, the explanation for this increase did not lie in the harder working conditions or the deterioration of our food supplies or a change of weather or new epidemics. It was simply that the majority of the prisoners had lived in the naïve hope that they would be home again by Christmas. As the time drew near and there was no encouraging news, the prisoners lost courage and disappointment overcame them. This had a dangerous influence on their powers of resistance and a great number of them died.

As we said before, any attempt to restore a man's inner strength in the camp had first to succeed in showing him some future goal. Nietzsche's words, "He who has a *why* to live for can bear with almost any *how*," could be the guiding motto for all psychotherapeutic and psychohygienic efforts regarding prisoners. Whenever there was an opportunity for it, one had to give them a why—an aim—for their lives, in order to strengthen them to bear the terrible *how* of their existence. Woe to him who saw no more sense in his life, no aim, no purpose, and therefore no point in carrying on. He was soon lost. The typical reply with which such a man rejected all encouraging arguments was, "I have nothing to expect from life any more." What sort of answer can one give to that?

What was really needed was a fundamental change in our attitude toward life. We had to learn ourselves and, furthermore, we had to teach the despairing men, that it did not really matter what we expected from life, but rather what life expected from us. We needed to stop asking about the meaning of life, and instead to think of ourselves as those who were being questioned by life—daily and hourly. Our answer must consist, not in talk and meditation, but in right action and in right conduct. Life ultimately means taking the responsibility to find the right answer to its problems and to fulfill the tasks which it constantly sets for each individual.

—Viktor E. Frankl, *Man's Search For Meaning*

11 · WHAT ARE PEOPLE GOOD FOR?

Ina Corinne Brown, who holds a Ph.D. degree from the University of Chicago, is professor of social anthropology at Scarritt College in Nashville, Tennessee. She is a tall, slender, gray-haired woman who thinks anthropology one of the most exciting subjects in the world because it deals with people—all kinds of people all over the world.

Dr. Brown has done research in the British Museum and Oxford University libraries and has traveled in Europe, the West Indies, Central Africa and the Orient. She is the author of several books, including *The Story of the American Negro* and *Race Relations in a Democracy*.

[She writes as follows.]

. . . .

One's beliefs are revealed not so much in words or in formal creeds as in the assumptions on which one habitually acts and in the basic values by which all choices are tested. The cornerstone of my own value system was laid in childhood by parents who believed that personal integrity came first. They never asked, "What will people think?" The question was, "W<u>hat will you think of yourself if you do this or fail to do that</u>?" Thus living up to one's own conception of oneself became a basic value and the question "What will people think?" took a subordinate place.

A second basic value, in some ways an extension of the first, I owe to an old college professor who had suffered more than his share of grief and trouble. Over and over he said to us: "<u>The one thing that really matters is to be bigger than the things that can happen to you. Nothing that can happen to you is half so important as the way in which you meet it.</u>"

Gradually I realized that here was the basis of the only real security and peace of mind that a human being can have. Nobody can be sure when disaster, disappointment, injustice or humiliation may come to him through no fault of his own. Nor can one be guaranteed against one's own mistakes and failures. But the way we meet life is ours to choose and when integrity, fortitude, dignity and compassion are our choice, the things that can happen to us lose their power over us.

The acceptance of these two basic values led to a third. If what one is and how one meets life are of first importance one is not impressed by another's money, status or power, nor does one judge people by their race, color or social position. This opens up a whole new world of relationships, for when friendships are based on qualities of mind and character one can have friends among old and young, rich and poor, famous and unknown, educated and unlettered, and among people of all races and all nations.

Given these three basic values, a fourth became inevitable. It is one's duty and obligation to help create a social order in which persons are more important than things, ideas more precious than gadgets, and in which individuals are judged on the basis of personal worth. Moreover, for this judgment to be fair human beings must have an opportunity for the fullest development of which they are capable. One is thus led to work for a world of freedom and justice through those social agencies and institutions which make it possible for people everywhere to realize their highest potentialities.

Perhaps all of this adds up to a belief in what has been called the human use of human beings. We are set off from the rest of the animal world by our capacity consciously to transcend our physical needs and desires. Men must concern themselves with food and with other physical needs, and they must protect themselves and their own from bodily harm, but these activities are not exclusively human. Many animals concern themselves with these things. When we worship, pray, or feel compassion, when we enjoy a painting, a sunset or a sonata, when we think and reason, pursue ideas, seek·truth, or read a book, when we protect the weak and helpless, when we honor the noble and cherish the good, when we co-operate with our fellow men to build a better world, our behavior is worthy of our status as human beings.

—Ina Corinne Brown, in *This I Believe*

CHAPTER 2—CHRISTIAN LIFE AND THE INNER LIFE

12 ·

—© 1967 United Feature Syndicate

13 · JOURNAL—MAY 24, 1738

13. I continued thus to seek it, (though with strange indifference, dullness, and coldness, and unusually frequent relapses into sin,) till Wednesday, May 24. I think it was about five this morning, that I opened my Testament on those words, . . . "There are given unto us exceeding great and precious promises, even that ye should be partakers of the divine nature." (2 Pet. i. 4.) Just as I went out, I opened it again on those words, "Thou are not far from the kingdom of God." In the afternoon I was asked to go to St. Paul's. The anthem was, "Out of the deep have I called unto thee, O Lord: Lord, hear my voice. O let thine ears consider well the voice of my complaint. If thou, Lord, wilt be extreme to mark what is done amiss, O Lord, who may abide it? For there is mercy with thee; therefore shalt thou be feared. O Israel, trust in the Lord: For with the Lord there is mercy, and with him is plenteous redemption. And He shall redeem Israel from all his sins."

14. In the evening I went very unwillingly to a society in Aldersgate-Street, where one was reading Luther's preface to the Epistle of the Romans. About a quarter before nine, while he was describing the change which God works in the heart through faith in Christ, I felt my heart strangely warmed. I felt I did trust in Christ, Christ alone for salvation: And an assurance was given me, that he had taken away *my* sins, even *mine,* and saved *me* from the law of sin and death.

15. I began to pray with all my might for those who had in a more especial manner despitefully used me and persecuted me. I then testified openly to all there, what I now first felt in my heart. But it was not long before the enemy suggested, "This cannot be faith; for where is thy joy?" Then was I taught, that peace and victory over sin are essential to faith in the Captain of our salvation: . . .

16. After my return home, I was much buffeted with temptations; but cried out, and they fled away. They returned again and again. I as often lifted up my eyes, and He "sent me help from his holy place." And herein I found the difference between this and my former state chiefly consisted. I was striving, yea, fighting with all my might under the law, as well as under grace. But then I was sometimes, if not often, conquered; now, I was always conqueror.

. . . .

Sat. 27—Believing one reason of my want of joy was want of time for prayer, I resolved to do no business till I went to church in the morning, but to continue pouring out my heart before Him. And this day my spirit was enlarged; so that though I was now also assaulted by many temptations, I was more than conqueror, gaining more power thereby to trust and to rejoice in God my Saviour.—John Wesley, *Works*

14 · HOW TO BECOME A NEW MAN

With some persons there may be in conversion an emotional crisis, the symptoms of which are similar to those of mental conflict. There may be deep feeling and outbursts of tears and anxiety. There may be none of these things. There are those who experience little, if any, emotion. They accept salvation without any particular crisis of mind or emotion. They cannot, in fact, specify any definite time when they first entered into their knowledge of Christ. My wife is one of the finest Christians I have ever known, but she cannot pinpoint the moment of her conversion. Yet she is sure of her conversion because she knows Christ personally in the reality of daily life and service, and she has the joy of the Lord.

When Jesus described the new birth to intellectual, dignified Nicodemus, He said: "The wind bloweth where it listeth, and thou hearest the sound thereof, but canst not tell whence it cometh, and whither it goeth: so is every one that is born of the Spirit" (Jn. 3:8). Jesus said it was like the movement of the wind, which sometimes is as imperceptible as a zephyr and at other times as revolutionary as a cyclone. Conversion is like that, too—sometimes quiet and tender, sometimes uprooting and rearranging the life under great emotional manifestation. —Billy Graham, *World Aflame*

15 · MOMENT OF DECISION

. . . We have said that there is no standard conversion experience; we have said that one man may accept Jesus Christ as Lord in one shattering moment, and that for another there may be an uninterrupted process and development. But in the difference there remains one common factor—there must in every life be some moment of decision.

In the one case it will be a moment in which the direction of life is even violently reversed, in which a man breaks with the old way and accepts the new. In the second case the decision will be a decision regarding the Church. . . . it will be a moment when he deliberately takes his stand beside the Christ whom he has known for long. It is not so much the acceptance of something new as it is the public and definite affirmation of something which has for long existed.

Here then comes the crux of the matter. In the one case it is the acceptance of Christ; in the other case it is deliberate, self-chosen entry into the Church. For very many the moment of decision will be the moment of the acceptance of full membership of the Church which is the body of Jesus Christ. If that be so, the moment of entry into Church membership should be the most decisive moment in a man's life. It should be an act of the most definite and far-reaching decision. 'All Christian apologetic,' Dr. Soper rightly says, 'breaks down unless it prompts those who speak and those who hear to a decision about Jesus Christ.'

—William Barclay, *Turning To God*

16 • LUTHER ON FAITH

Faith is not so easy a matter as pope and enthusiastic fanatics dream it is. I am a Doctor of Holy Scripture and have now studied the lesson of faith for twenty years and have also preached to others about it. Nevertheless, when the sun burns down upon me and temptation comes along, I feel and find that I droop and wilt, as grass in the heat and drought. And if God did not refresh me with His rain and dew, that is, with His Word and Spirit, I should have to wither away. . . . God's Spirit and power, constant practice and experience, are required to arrive at the point at which I ride above all things, despise sin and death, and with all confidence cheerfully rely on God's promise.—*What Luther Says* (Ewald M. Plass, Ed.)

17 • FAITH AS RESONANCE

Let us begin by describing faith as resonance, that dimension of reality in every event and thing which provides the possibility of reverberating to the sound of other events and other things. There is a resonance between man and the world; they are not only related, they are dynamically moved by each other; they hear each other. There is a resonance between the spirit and the flesh; each causes reverberations in the other, and thus spirit sanctifies the flesh, while flesh makes the spirit real. There is a resonance between God and the world; they fulfill each other, God speaking through the world, and the world finding its answer in God. At every level of life, in all events and circumstances, resonance is the reality of a ubiquitous relationship by which the world may be reconciled to God.

—Samuel H. Miller, *The Dilemma of Modern Belief*

18 · WHEN A MAN GETS PULLED OUT

[John 3:1-21 as translated by underprivileged children and youth.]

One night a man hunted out Jesus.
  He said, "I got the feeling that you're on the level
    And you don't give us the go round."

Jesus said,
  "Right, man.
    Unless a man gets pulled out he will never see God."

So Nicodemus said,
  "So what do you want me to do,
    Fall in the creek and wait for a cat to pull me out?
      Man! what if he don't come along?"

Jesus says,
  "No, no, no,
    I'm not talking about the creek
    I mean the way you're drifting, man.

You're always getting into trouble
  And all that jazz.
    To knock that off is what I mean."

When you're in the alley you hear the trucks.
  You can't tell what street they are on
    Or where they are going, right?
      But the trucker knows where he's going.

That's how it is when you get pulled out.
  You act like you know where you're going
    And you do know where you're going
    And you don't drop out.

Then Jesus came right out with it and said,
  "God loved everybody
    So much that he sent his son, Jesus,
      To pull us out
        So we would always know where we
        are going."
                    —Carl F. Burke, *God Is for Real, Man*

19 · THE FOUNDATION OF HOPE

One of the most eloquent statements of the meaning of hope is from the pen of John Calvin (*Institutes of Religion,* III.2.42):

> In short, hope is no other than the expectations of those things which faith has believed to be truly promised by God. Thus faith believes the veracity of God, hope expects the manifestation of it in due time; faith believes him to be our Father, hope expects him always to act towards us in this character; faith believes that eternal life is given to us, hope expects it one day to be revealed; faith is the foundation on which hope rests, hope nourishes and sustains faith.

Our hope rests in God and his purposes, not in our ability to build his kingdom or to predict the time and form of its coming. In Jesus Christ, God has come to us from out of eternity to reveal his nature and purpose, to unleash within our world the power of his Spirit by which the principalities and powers that hinder his purposes may be defeated. Through Jesus Christ, God has called us into the fellowship and the common tasks of those engaged in the ministry of reconciliation, whereby all men and the whole of creation are summoned to submit to God's sovereign will and purpose for his creation. By the resurrection of Jesus Christ, God has shown his power to overcome death and to deliver man from his ultimate enemy. It is in the power of the God who raises from the dead that we are commissioned to assume our share in the work by which God purposes to reconcile the world to himself. —Howard Clark Kee, *The Renewal of Hope*

20 · EXPERIENCES IN A CONCENTRATION CAMP

[Viktor Frankl lived through the hopelessness of the World War II concentration camps. The bestiality of camp life stripped prisoners down "to naked existence." Most of his family, including his wife, died in prison or in the gas ovens.]

. . . It is a peculiarity of man that he can only live by looking to the future. . . . And this is his salvation in the most difficult moments of his existence, although he sometimes has to force his mind to the task.

I remember a personal experience. Almost in tears from pain (I had terrible sores on my feet from wearing torn shoes), I limped a few kilometers with our long column of men from the camp to our work site. Very cold, bitter winds struck us. I kept thinking of the endless little problems of our miserable life. What would there be to eat tonight? If a piece of sausage came as extra ration, should I exchange it for a piece of bread? Should I trade my last cigarette, which was left from a bonus I received a fortnight ago, for a bowl of soup? How could I get a piece of wire to replace the fragment which served as one of my shoelaces? Would I get to our work site in time to join my usual working party or would I have to join another, which might have a brutal foreman? What could I do to get on good terms with the Capo [prisoners who acted as trustees, having special privileges], who could help me to obtain work in camp instead of undertaking this horribly long daily march?

I became disgusted with the state of affairs which compelled me, daily and hourly, to think of only such trivial things. I forced my thoughts to turn to another subject. Suddenly I saw myself standing on the platform of a well-lit, warm and pleasant lecture room. In front of me sat an attentive audience on comfortable upholstered seats. I was giving a lecture on the psychology of the concentration camp! All that oppressed me at that moment became objective, seen and described from the remote viewpoint of science. By this method I succeed somehow in rising above the situation, above the sufferings of the moment, and I observed them as if they were already of the past. Both I and my troubles became the object of an interesting psychoscientific study undertaken by myself. What does Spinoza say in his Ethics? . . . Emotion, which is suffering, ceases to be suffering as soon as we form a clear and precise picture of it.—Viktor E. Frankl, *Man's Search For Meaning*

21 · A PRAYER

Lord—

> I've been talking with you for a long time.
> I've been trying to listen, too.
> I've thought about the action, Lord,

>   But that's not quite so easy!
>   It means involvement!
>   It means insecurity!
>   It means turmoil
>   in my well-ordered life!
>
> Lord—
>   I guess I've had myself
>   at the center of all of this.
>   And it has to be YOU, Lord.
>
> I've been thinking of MY world, Lord—
>   But it's really your world, Lord.
>
> I've sensed that YOU understand ME, Lord,
>   But do I understand YOU?
>
> Things are a mess in this world, Lord.
>
>   But they were a mess when
>   You were here, too, Lord.
>
>   Together
>   can
>   we really
>   do something
>   about it?
> —Ruth and Arthayer Sanborn, *Do You Hear Me, God?*

22 · HEREIN IS LOVE

Jesus Christ stands between the lover and the others he loves. I do not know in advance what love of others means on the basis of the general idea of love that grows out of my human desires—all this may rather be hatred and an insidious kind of selfishness in the eyes of Christ. What love is, only Christ tells in his Word. Contrary to all my own opinions and convictions, Jesus Christ will tell me what love toward the brethren really is. Therefore, spiritual love is bound solely to the Word of Jesus Christ. Where Christ bids me to maintain fellowship for the sake of love, I will maintain it. Where his truth enjoins me to dissolve a fellowship for love's sake, there I will dissolve it, despite all the protests of my human love. Because spiritual love does not desire but rather serves, it loves an enemy as a brother. It originates neither in the brother nor in the enemy but in Christ and his Word. Human love can never understand spiritual love, for spiritual love is from above; it is something completely strange, new, and incomprehensible to all earthly love.

Because Christ stands between me and others, I dare not desire direct fellowship with them. As only Christ can speak to me in such a way that I may be saved, so others, too, can be saved only by Christ himself. This means that I must release the other person from every attempt of mine to regulate, coerce, and dominate him with my love. The other person needs to retain his independence of me; to be loved for what he is, as one for whom Christ became man, died, and rose again, for whom Christ bought forgiveness of sins and eternal life. . . . —Dietrich Bonhoeffer, *Life Together*

23 · ACT LIKE A MAN

. . . The most important thing for man to do here is not to obey God's specific will or commands, but to accept his own freedom and responsibility to be a man, a center of creativity, an initiator of relationships, a maker of things. Until man takes responsibility for what he does specifically

THE INNER LIFE

instead of saying that God told him to do it, there is no way for man to "serve" God. God is not interested in man's being any less a man in order to be a Christian. Man is not a man in order to be a Christian, but he is a Christian in order to be a man. This is, his concept of humanness is given him in Christian faith. His freedom to act in full responsibility and dignity is a gift Christ bestows upon him. God is no more interested in giving specific instructions to men than parents are to mature children. His will is not in his "words" but in his "Word." Here the answer is no longer, "you should vote democratic," or "you should marry Jim," or "you should keep Red China out of the United Nations." Rather it is, "consider all the factors in the situation and do what seems to you best to serve the welfare of all the persons involved, remembering my love for you whether the choice is right or not." God's relation to man brings to expression a similar kind of trust. But the specific decision is man's, not God's, a decision taken within love, freedom, trust, and responsibility. The entire process is open to the dimension of the Holy, but the Holy is not localized so as to bear responsibility for man's specific decisions. Every decision is taken within faith and yet man accepts full responsibility for the decision. . . .

—Jack Boozer & William A. Beardslee, *Faith to Act*

CHAPTER 3—THE INNER FREEDOM TO BE ONESELF

24 · I WAS GYPPED

The lips are curved into an obliging, fixed half-smile. The grey hair is coiffured with mathematical precision, cleft exactly by the part. At the neck, not entirely masked by the photographer's shadows, a few age lines can be discerned. . . .

. . . Simone de Beauvoir has no husband and no children; by design, she has denied herself the rewards, or the burdens, of maternity. The smile is unreal, put on, perhaps, for the photographer; she cannot accept or endure the fact that she is now 57. Her mortality has obsessed her for a generation. "Since 1944, the most important, the most irreparable thing that has happened to me is that I have grown old. How is it that time, which has no form or substance, can crush me with so huge a weight that I can no longer breathe?"

. . . .

... She was the Mother Hubbard of existentialism, a clock in a refrigerator, a cerebral Joan of Arc—to cite some of the appellations, largely invidious, that were flung at her during her prime. Periodically, she issued books, all of them painstakingly analytical and exhaustingly long. . . .

. . . .

... Simone de Beauvoir attained everything that she ever aspired to as a girl: celebrity as a writer, the full exercise of her rebel spirit. Nevertheless, at 57, she finds herself "hostile to the society to which I belonged, banished by my age from the future, stripped fiber by fiber from my past."

"If it had at least enriched the earth," she writes, summing up her life. "If it had given birth to . . . what? A hill? A rocket? The promises have all been kept. And yet, turning an incedulous gaze toward that young and credulous girl, I realize with stupor how much I was gypped." —*Time*

25 · TRAPPED?

... It is worth acknowledging that one of the most ominous features of contemporary life is the feeling of fatalism on the part of the individual. He tends to assume that his future lies wholly in the hands of forces which he cannot direct at all, or can influence only to an insignificant degree. This assumption reflects another one, namely, that what determines his security or insecurity, his success or failure, the worth or futility of his life, is something outside himself. He is at the mercy of fortune. Modern man's substitute for Fate is largely to be found in those dehumanized mass forces which sweep peoples into depressions, totalitarianism and war. The greatest threat to human existence is no longer nature; to an enormous extent science has made it possible to use nature for human ends. The greatest threat is man himself—his untamed irrational drives, his cruelty, his capacity for collective self-deception and mistrust.

Among the expedients available, aside from "education," there are only two which can *directly* transform man's internal character-structure; only two which can thus assist him to bring forth from within himself the resources for changing the patterns of contemporary civilization. Those two resources are psychotherapy and religion. Quite conceivably they may not succeed. Indeed, it is somewhat ironical that psychologists, anthropologists and sociologists are reaching conclusions about how to *design* a culture intelligently at the very moment when rapidly moving events may forever shut off the opportunity for putting their knowledge into practice.

Whether world civilization survives the present crisis or not, the stress upon the word "directly" in the above statement is necessary because under pressing circumstances men show an amazing capacity for unplanned, undirected adaptation. They can make adjustments to new and staggeringly different modes of life, which lead to profound changes in character and motivation, without deliberately attempting to alter themselves inwardly at all. Unless there were these hidden resources for meeting emergencies human life probably would have vanished from the planet long ago. . . .

—David E. Roberts
Psychotherapy and a Christian View of Man

26 · HUMAN RESOURCES FOR SELF-POSSESSION

... We seek answers to the meaning of life by means of acquiring wealth, power, pleasure, popularity and any number of other things. All of these things, so long as they are external, leave us at the mercy of circumstances and in the power of others. If the basis for the worth of a man's existence does not lie within him, then the significance of his life can be destroyed by forces beyond his control. The net result is deepseated anxiety. Such anxiety may cause endless attempts to tighten one's grip upon property and power; but these expedients can do no more than evade the problem; they cannot eradicate it. Usually, the more desperately one places one's eggs in such baskets, the more vulnerable he is. Feverish effort may drive a sense of emptiness and lostness out of consciousness; but the emptiness is therefore all the more acute at the core. The disruption is sure to be serious once strategies for keeping the emptiness out of sight have broken down. This sense of emptiness, lostness and isolation, which is so prevalent in contemporary life, is symptomatic of the fact that human resources for self-possession are not being adequately employed. Far too often we strive to meet the problem by *having* something significant instead of by *becoming or being* something significant. —David E. Roberts
Psychotherapy and a Christian View of Man

27 · FROM EDWARD KENNEDY'S TRIBUTE TO HIS BROTHER

"It is a revolutionary world which we live in, and this generation at home and around the world has had thrust upon it a greater burden of responsibility than any generation that has ever lived. Some believe there is nothing one man or one woman can do against the enormous array of the world's ills. Yet many of the world's great movements of thought and action have flowed from the work of a single man.

"A young monk began the Protestant Reformation. A young general extended an empire from Macedonia to the borders of the earth. A young woman reclaimed the territory of France, and it was a young Italian explorer who discovered the New World, and the 32-year-old Thomas Jefferson who explained that all men are created equal.

"These men moved the world, and so can we all. Few will have the greatness to bend history itself, but each of us can work to change a small portion of events, and in the total of all those acts will be written the history of this generation.

"Each time a man stands for an ideal, or acts to improve the lot of others, or strikes out against injustice, he sends forth a tiny ripple of hope.

"And crossing each other from a million different centers of energy and daring, those ripples build a current that can sweep down the mightiest walls of oppression and resistance. Few are willing to brave the disapproval of their fellows, the censure of their colleagues, the wrath of their society. Moral courage is a rarer commodity than bravery in battle or great intelligence. Yet it is the one essential vital quality for those who seek to change a world that yields most painfully to change.

"And I believe that in this generation those with the courage to enter the moral conflict will find themselves with companions in every corner of the globe.

"For the fortunate among us there is the temptation to follow the easy and familiar paths of personal ambition and financial success so grandly spread before those who enjoy the privilege of education. But that is not the road history has marked out for us.

"Like it or not, we live in times of danger and uncertainty. But they are also more open to the creative energy of men than any other time in history. All of us will ultimately be judged and as the years pass, we will surely judge ourselves, on the effort we have contributed to building a new world society and the extent to which our ideals and goals have shaped that event.

"Our future may lie beyond our vision, but it is not completely beyond our control. It is the shaping impulse of America that neither faith nor nature nor the irresistible tides of history but the work of our own hands matched to reason and principle will determine our destiny."

—*The New York Times*

28 · SOME LIMITS TO FREEDOM

... The inorganic world may be compared to a train which is compelled by the rigid rails on which it runs to follow exactly a pre-established course. The world of living things, on the other hand, is like a motor-car which enjoys a certain margin of deviation from side to side on the road. Its course is kept practically straight by means of continual corrections to right or left applied through the steering wheel. Without this regulation the car would finish up in the ditch. But the regulation is a supple one, needing an intelligent driver, not an inflexible rail.

. . . .

... If he [the intelligent driver] is accustomed to driving, he controls the progress of his vehicle quite automatically, through acquired reflexes. But when he arrives at a cross-roads, his action in turning the steering-wheel to take the road on the left or the right is of quite a different sort. He exercises his will to make a conscious decision.

Thus we have the same driver, making the same movement with his steering-wheel, but this time the significance of his action is of quite a different order. In the first case his action is automatic and recurrent; in the second it is an isolated act of the will. . . .—Paul Tournier, *The Meaning of Persons*

29 · OUR DECISIONS AND OUR FREEDOM

... We might begin our discussion with one concrete, commonplace example: the freedom of choice between smoking or not smoking. Let us take a heavy smoker who has read the reports on the health hazards of smoking and has arrived at the conclusion that he wants to stop smoking. He has "decided that he is going to stop." This "decision" is no decision. It is nothing but the formulation of a hope. He has "decided" to stop smoking, yet the next day he feels in too good a mood, the day after in too bad a mood, the third day he does not want to appear "asocial," the following day he doubts that the health reports are correct, and so he continues smoking, although he had "decided" to stop. All these decisions are nothing but ideas, plans, fantasies; they have little or no reality until the real choice is made. This choice becomes real when he has a cigarette in front of him and has to decide whether to smoke *this* cigarette or not; again, later he has to decide about another cigarette, and so on. It is always the concrete act which requires a decision. The question in each such situation is whether he is free not to smoke, or whether he is not free.

Several questions arise here. Assuming he did not believe in the health reports on smoking or, even if he did, he is convinced that it is better to live twenty years less than to miss this pleasure; in this case there is apparently no problem of choice. Yet the problem may only be camouflaged. His con-

scious thoughts may be nothing but rationalizations of his feeling that he could not win the battle even if he tried; hence he may prefer to pretend that there is no battle to win. But whether the problem of choice is conscious or unconscious, the nature of the choice is the same. It is the choice between an action which is dictated by reason as against an action which is dictated by irrational passions. . . .
—Erich Fromm, *The Heart Of Man*

30 • "SOMETHING" DOES NOT GIVE UP ON US

Often the profoundest form of faith comes to a man only when, despite the fact that he has given up on himself, "something" does not give up on him. Positive faith has not been reached so long as despair predominates; but, in our age especially, many of us cannot find a faith that will stand up except by passing through despair and receiving a stable orientation toward life—cleansed of illusions and defensiveness—on the other side. When that happens the work of healing power (grace) which bestows beatitude as a gift (though not without participation on our part), has a compelling and inescapable quality that is utterly different from the "You *must* believe" of authoritarian threats. In the latter case the individual finds himself under the pressure of demands which override his freedom; in the former case, he finds himself captured by a healing power which enhances his freedom. —David E. Roberts
Psychotherapy and a Christian View of Man

31 • GOD'S GRACE AND HUMAN FREEDOM

. . . The moralist must hold his breath and keep his muscles tense; and so long as this athletic attitude is possible all goes well—morality suffices. But the athletic attitude tends ever to break down, and it inevitably does break down even in the most stalwart when the organism begins to decay, or when morbid fears invade the mind. . . . What he craves is to be consoled in his very powerlessness, to feel that the spirit of the universe recognizes and secures him, all decaying and failing as he is. Well, we are all such helpless failures in the last resort. The sanest and best of us are of one clay with lunatics and prison inmates, and death finally runs the robustest of us down. And whenever we feel this, such a sense of the vanity and provisionality of our voluntary career comes over us that all our morality appears but as a plaster hiding a sore it can never cure, and all our well-doing as the hollowest substitute for that well-*being* that our lives ought to be grounded in, but, alas! are not.

And here religion comes to our rescue and takes our fate into her hands. There is a state of mind, known to religious men, but to no others, in which the will to assert ourselves and hold our own has been displaced by a willingness to close our mouths and be as nothing in the floods and waterspouts of God. In this state of mind, what we most dreaded has become the habitation of our safety, and the hour of our moral death has turned into our spiritual birthday. The time for tension in our soul is over, and that of happy relaxation, of calm deep breathing, of an eternal present, with no discordant future to be anxious about, has arrived. Fear is not held in abeyance as it is by mere morality, it is positively expunged and washed away.

. . . We shall see how infinitely passionate a thing religion at its highest flights can be. Like love, like wrath, like hope, ambition, jealousy, like every other instinctive eagerness and impulse, it adds to life an enchantment which is not rationally or logically deducible from anything else. This enchantment, coming as a gift when it does come—a gift of our organism, the physiologists will tell us, a gift of God's grace, the theologians say—is either there or not there for us, and there are persons who can no more become possessed by it than they can fall in love with a given woman by mere word of command. Religious feeling is thus an absolute addition to the Subject's range of life. It gives him a new sphere of power. When the outward battle is lost, and the outer world disowns him, it redeems and vivifies an interior world which otherwise would be an empty waste.

If religion is to mean anything definite for us, it seems to me that we ought to take it as meaning this added dimension of emotion, this enthusiastic temper of espousal, in regions where morality strictly so called can at best but bow its head and acquiesce. It ought to mean nothing short of this new reach of freedom for us, with the struggle over, the keynote of the universe sounding in our ears, and everlasting possession spread before our eyes.

This sort of happiness in the absolute and everlasting is what we find nowhere but in religion. . . .

—William James, *The Varieties of Religious Experience*

32 · THE YOKE OF RELIGION

. . . We are all laboring under the yoke of religion; we all, sometimes, try to throw away old or new doctrines or dogmas, but after a little while we return, again enslaving ourselves and others in their servitude.

The same is true of the practical laws of religion. They demand ritual activities, the participation in religious enterprises and the study of religious traditions, prayer, sacraments and meditations. They demand moral obedience, inhuman self-control and asceticism, devotion to man and things beyond our possibilities, surrender to ideas and duties beyond our power, unlimited self-negation, and unlimited self-perfection: the religious law demands the perfect in all respects. And our conscience agrees with this demand. But the split in our being is derived from just this: that the perfect, although it is the truth, is beyond us, against us, judging and condemning us. So we try to throw away the ritual and moral demands. We neglect them, we hate them, we criticize them; some of us display a cynical indifference toward the religious and moral law. But since mere cynicism is as impossible as mere scepticism, we return to old or new laws, becoming more fanatic than ever before, and take a yoke of the law upon us, which is more self-defying, more cruel against ourselves, and more willing to coerce other people under the same yoke in the name of the perfect. Jesus Himself becomes for these perfectionists, puritans and moralists a teacher of the religious law putting upon us the heaviest of all burdens, the burden of *His* law. But that is the greatest possible distortion of the mind of Jesus. This distortion can be found in the minds of those who crucified Him because He broke the religious law, not by fleeing from it like the cynical Sadducees, but by overcoming it. We are all permanently in danger of abusing Jesus by stating that He is the founder of a new religion, and the bringer of another, more refined, and more enslaving law. And so we see in all Christian Churches the toiling and laboring of people who are called Christians, serious Christians, under innumerable laws which they cannot fulfill, from which they flee, to which they return, or which they replace by other laws. This is the yoke from which Jesus wants to liberate us. . . .

—Paul Tillich, *The Shaking of the Foundations*

33 · OPENING CHANNELS FOR GOD'S GRACE

Prayer, which means the knowledge of God by firsthand *acquaintance* rather than by mere *description,* is a turning away from self to the Divine Companion. The purpose of prayer is not to change God's intention, which is already perfectly loving, but rather, by some mysterious process, which in our finiteness we cannot understand, to open channels of grace and power which otherwise are closed. If you can turn to God, at anytime of day or night, as naturally and unpretentiously as a child turning to his mother, you have found the secret of the saints.

—Elton Trueblood, *The Life We Prize*

34 · FREE WILL

... Because God is a Father who wants children who are true persons, he has given us a small amount of independent power in our self-conscious free wills. ...

... I have the same relationship with my tropical fish that God has with man. I have total power and responsibility over them in their fragile aquariums. I see to it that they get water, food, heat, light, medicine, plants, aeration, and sanitation. I can permit them to swim about, or I can catch them in a net and transfer them to another aquarium. My fish are completely in my power. Thus, from their "fishes' eye" point of view, I am, comparatively speaking, their almighty god.

But even these little fish have a type of free will, a power to cooperate or not to cooperate with me. Within the confines of their glass walls they can swim wherever they wish, run from me or toward me, fight each other or love each other, and so forth. They can, and usually do, flick their tails at me and hide behind a rock or a plant when they see me approaching with a net. In the same fashion, man is insignificant in God's sight when we compare our might to his. But we are still independent persons who can resist the Almighty Creator himself if we so wish.

—J. Schoneberg Setzer, *What's Left to Believe?*

35 · BE A CHRIST TO YOUR NEIGHBOR

Joseph had to do his best, and it may well be that he asked some maid to fetch water or something else, but we do not read that anyone came to help. They heard that a young wife was lying in a cow stall and no one gave heed. Shame on you, wretched Bethlehem! The inn ought to have been burned with brimstone, for even though Mary had been a beggar maid or unwed, anybody at such a time should have been glad to give her a hand.

There are many of you in this congregation who think to yourselves: "If only I had been there! How quick I would have been to help the Baby! I would have washed his linen. How happy I would have been to go with the shepherds to see the Lord lying in the manger!" Yes, you would! You say that because you know how great Christ is, but if you had been there at that time you would have done no better than the people of Bethlehem. Childish and silly thoughts are these! Why don't you do it now? You have Christ in your neighbor. You ought to serve him, for what you do to your neighbor in need you do to the Lord Christ himself.

—Martin Luther, *The Martin Luther Christmas Book*

CHAPTER 4—HOW AND WHERE FAITH GROWS

36 · GOD GIVES GROWTH

[I Corinthians 3:6-8a]. Paul had begun the work at Corinth. The use of the term "watering" in connection with Apollos does not mean that he had made no new converts; Paul is simply referring to the second stage in promoting growth. Yet human effort is never the real source of a spiritual result. As in Jesus' parables of growth (Mark 4:26-29), the emphasis

lies not on what man has done in sowing, but on that which is outside his power and depends upon God alone. All man's labor would be in vain if God did not cause the seed to grow. . . .
—Clarence Tucker Craig, in *The Interpreter's Bible*

37 · RESPONSIBILITY AND INDEPENDENCE

The child's inner emotional reaction to our instruction is a decisive element in how much he learns of what we want him to know. Values cannot be taught directly. They are absorbed, and become part of the child, only through his identification with, and emulation of, persons who gain his love and respect.

Thus, the problem of responsibility in children is referred back to the parent, or more precisely to the parent's values as expressed in his child-rearing practices. The question to consider now is: Are there any definite attitudes and practices that are likely to create a desired sense of responsibility in our children? . . .

. . . .

Responsibility in children starts with the parent's attitude and skills. The attitudes include a willingness to allow children to feel *all* their feelings; the skills include an ability to demonstrate to children acceptable way of coping with feelings.

The difficulties entailed in meeting these two requirements are most formidable. Our own parents and teachers have not adequately prepared us for dealing with emotions. They themselves did not know how to cope with strong feelings. When confronted with turbulent emotions in children, they tried to deny, disown, suppress, or prettify them. They used pat phrases that were not too helpful:

Denial: You don't really mean what you say; you know you love your little brother.

Disowning: It's not you, it's the devil in you that is acting up.

Suppression: If you mention the word "hate" once more, you'll get the spanking of your life. A nice child does not feel like that.

Prettifying: You don't really hate your brother. Maybe you dislike him. You should rise above such feelings.

Such statements ignore the fact that emotions, like rivers, cannot be stopped, only diverted. Strong feelings, like the rising waters of the Mississippi, cannot be denied, reasoned with, or talked out of, existence. To attempt to ignore them is to invite disaster. They must be recognized and their power acknowledged. They must be treated with respect and diverted with ingenuity. Thus channeled, they may electrify our existence and bring light and joy into our lives.

—Haim G. Ginott, *Between Parent and Child*

38 · DISENFRANCHISED PEOPLE

[The underground church, a small group within the Church seeking renewal, in Philadelphia, Pennsylvania, engages in dialogue with both the established Church and the culture. Could the following dialogue about disenfranchised people be exchanged in other areas of our culture?]

. . . Many spokesmen for disenfranchised, disenchanted Black people have come to understand that racism in America is all-pervasive. They have at last seen the basic truths in the still-continued repression and humiliation of themselves by White people: truths of racial bigotry, class separation, political irresponsibility to constituent citizens, and the immorality of our social apathy. In short, such Black anger has its documentable rationale . . . and it wants no truck with any member (not just with the representatives) of that power structure which preserves, if not actually nourishes, such horrors. So it is that the militant White revolutionary is rejected by the very people who have guided him to question ineffective and dishonest Churches. . . .

—Layton P. Zimmer, in *The Underground Church*

39 · THE CHURCH AS CHAPLAIN AND TEACHER

. . . In the mythology of American culture the task of moral guidance has been conferred on the Church, the home, and the school. The obvious explanation for moral decline today is that the Church, the home, and the school are no longer "doing their job." It may be too simple a diagnosis, but it reflects a popular wisdom too often ignored by the specialists who seek to minister to contemporary ills.

The schools are increasingly trapped in a structural milieu, aided and abetted by administrative myopia, that leads to what Paul Goodman has called "compulsory miseducation." Imaginative teachers are often the first to sense the limitations of a system which overcrowds classrooms, burdens frontline educators with back-room bureaucratic form filling, and refuses to demand enough money to do the job that needs doing.

In many cases the home has held up well. It is the most decentralized institution in society. Even within a standardized environment it can set its own standards. If anything, the breakdown of the family may be the result of its having to do too much rather than too little. It must often serve as community, disciplinarian, creative environment, bastion of privacy, center of intimacy, economic provider, and cultural guide in order to fill the void created by a lack of community, culture, and decent relationships in the wider world. Whatever the causes, the divorce statistics, if they can be believed, provide an alarming index of the family's inability to remain stable, and of the parent's difficulty in exercising positive influence on their children.

One senses that if a breakdown in Church, home, and school continues, the total society will either be the locus of revolutionary upheaval, or the state will gradually assume more and more authority. The problems to date have seemed greater than the proposed solutions. Nevertheless, revolution is a last resort, and the prospect of vastly increased state domination is not a happy one. The effort to renew existing structures and to create new ones where present forms are obsolete becomes the only responsible strategy.

—Stephen C. Rose, *The Grass Roots Church*

40 · TRUE INTERGROUP RELATIONS

There are those Christians who agree that racism is a moral evil but advocate prudence in removing it from society. They fear losing people as Church members; they fear losing money. If preaching the message of justice and brotherhood and the condemnation of racism means that half of our congregations are going to stop coming to church on Sunday, we will lose millions of dollars. But perhaps the Church has to die, perhaps it has to be crucified, in order to experience resurrection.

The members of the Milwaukee Youth Council have been a source of inspiration to me because of their courage, because they are "shock troops" in the cause of love and justice. They always take the lead. During the early days of our open-housing demonstrations they were literally almost killed. We have all been in jail; we have all eaten tear gas. As the demonstrations progressed, as we were marching and singing to-

gether, we were growing in our relationship as brothers. White people and Black people were growing. In true intergroup relations, a person never ceases to grow. And the more we grow in brotherhood, the more we grow in the Spirit, for brotherhood and life in the Spirit, like the spiritual and temporal orders, are inseparable.
—James E. Groppie, in *The Underground Church*

41 · A PRAYER

Eternal and everblessed God, we remember this day the unseen cloud of witnesses who compass us about. We remember the blessed dead who do rest from their labours, and whose works do follow them. And we give Thee thanks for all of them.

For parents who gave us life; who tended and cared for us in years when we were helpless to help ourselves; who toiled and sacrificed to give to us our chance in life; at whose knees we learned to pray, and from whose lips we first heard the name of Jesus:
    We give Thee thanks, O God.

For teachers who taught us;
For ministers of Thy gospel who instructed us in Thy truth and in Thy faith;
For all those who have been an example to us of what life should be;
For those whose influence on us will never cease, and whose names will never depart from our memory;
    We give Thee thanks, O God.

For the saints, the prophets and the martyrs;
For those who lived and died for the faith;

And, above all else, for Jesus, the captain of our salvation
and the author and finisher of our faith:
We give Thee thanks, O God.

Grant unto us in our day and generation to walk worthily
of the heritage into which we have entered: through Jesus
Christ our Lord. AMEN.
—William Barclay, *A Book of Everyday Prayers*

42 · KIM, CABIN BOY AND SEAMAN

The press bureau of the chief of the SS and the police force in Denmark on Sunday, April 8, 1945, issued the following announcement:

> Condemned to death: Seaman Kim Malthe-Bruun, born July 8, 1923, in Saskatchewan, Canada, resident in Copenhagen, because, as a member of an illegal organization, he possessed himself of a revenue service boat and took it to Sweden. In addition he procured arms for his organization and took part in transporting arms. The death sentence was carried out by a firing squad.

. . . .

Farewell Letter to His Mother
Western Prison, German Section, Cell 411
April 4, 1945

Dear Mother: Today, together with Jörgen, Nils, and Ludwig, I was arraigned before a military tribunal. We were condemned to death. I know that you are a courageous woman, and that you will bear this, but, hear me, it is not enough to bear it, you must also understand it. I am an insignificant thing, and my person will soon be forgotten, but the thought, the life, the inspiration that filled me will live on. You will meet them everywhere—in the trees at springtime, in people who cross your path, in a loving little smile. You will encounter that something which perhaps had value in me, you will cherish it, and you will not forget me. And so I shall have a chance to grow, to become large and mature. I shall be living with all of you whose hearts I once filled. And you will all live on, knowing that I have preceded you, and not, as perhaps you thought at first, dropped out behind you. You know what my dearest wish has always been, and what I hoped to become. Follow me, my dear mother, on my path, and do not stop before the end, but linger with some of the matters belonging to the last space of time allotted to me, and you will find something that may be of value both to my sweetheart and to you, my mother.

I travelled a road that I have never regretted. I have never evaded the dictate of my heart, and now things seem to fall into place. I am not old, I should not be dying, yet it seems so natural to me, so simple. It is only the abrupt manner of it that frightens us at first. The time is short, I cannot properly explain it, but my soul is perfectly at rest. . . .

When I come right down to it, how strange it is to be sitting here and writing this testament. Every word must stand, it can never be amended, erased, or changed. I have so many thoughts. Jörgen is sitting here before me writing his two-year-old daughter a letter for her confirmation. A document for life. He and I have lived together, and now we die together, two comrades. . . .

I see the course that things are taking in our country, and I know that grandfather will prove to have been right, but remember—and all of you must remember this—that your dream must not be to return to the time before the war, but that all of you, young and old, should create conditions that are not arbitrary but that will bring to realization a genuinely human ideal, something that every person will see and feel to be an ideal for all of us. That is the great gift for which our country thirsts—something for which every humble peasant boy can yearn, and which he can joyously feel himself to have a part in and to be working for.

Finally, there is the girl whom I call mine. Make her realize that the stars still shine and that I have been only a milestone on her road. Help her on: she can still become very happy.

In haste—your eldest child and only son,
Kim
Dying We Live
(Helmut Gollwitzer, Käthe Kuhn, Reinhold Schneider, Ed.)

43 ·

"*If you think I'm going to worship that, you're out of your mind!*"
—Copyright 1966 Saturday Review, Inc.

44 · OUT OF OUR EXPERIENCE WITH JESUS

We are experiencing what Paul experienced. In the very moment when we were coming nearer to the historical Jesus than men had ever come before, and were already stretching out our hands to draw Him into our own time, we have been obliged to give up the attempt and acknowledge our failure in that paradoxical saying: "If we have known Christ after the flesh yet henceforth know we Him no more." And further we must be prepared to find that the historical knowledge of the personality and life of Jesus will not be a help, but perhaps even an offence to religion.

But the truth is, it is not Jesus as historically known, but Jesus as spiritually arisen within men, who is significant for our time and can help it. Not the historical Jesus but the spirit which goes forth from Him and in the spirits of men strives for new influence and rule, is that which overcomes the world.

. . . .

But in reality that which is eternal in the words of Jesus is due to the very fact that they are based on an eschatological worldview, and contain the expression of a mind for which the contemporary world with its historical and social circumstances no longer had any existence. They are appropriate, therefore, to any world, for in every world they raise the man who dares to meet their challenge, and does not turn and twist them into meaninglessness, above his world and his time, making him inwardly free, so that he is fitted to be, in his own world and in his own time, a simple channel of the power of Jesus.

. . . .

For that reason it is a good thing that the true historical Jesus should overthrow the modern Jesus, should rise up against the modern spirit and send upon earth, not peace, but a sword. He was not teacher, not a casuist; He was an imperious ruler. It was because He was so in His inmost being that He could think of Himself as the Son of Man. That was only the temporally conditioned expression of the fact that He was an authoritative ruler. The names in which men expressed their recognition of Him as such, Messiah, Son of Man, Son of God, have become for us historical parables. We can find no designation which expresses what He is for us.

He comes to us as One unknown, without a name, as of old, by the lake-side, He came to those men who knew Him not. He speaks to us the same word: "Follow thou me!" and sets us to the tasks which He has to fulfill for our time. He commands. And to those who obey Him, whether they be wise or simple, He will reveal Himself in the toils, the conflicts, the sufferings which they shall pass through in His fellowship, and, as an ineffable mystery, they shall learn in their own experience Who He is.

—Albert Schweitzer, *The Quest of the Historical Jesus*

45 · A KNOCK AT MIDNIGHT

At the beginning of the bus boycott in Montgomery, Alabama, we set up a voluntary car pool to get the people to and from their jobs. For eleven long months our car pool functioned extraordinarily well. Then Mayor Gayle introduced a resolution instructing the city's legal department to file such proceedings as it might deem proper to stop the operation of the car pool or any transportation system growing out of the bus boycott. A hearing was set for Tuesday, November 13, 1956.

At our regular weekly mass meeting, scheduled the night before the hearing, I had the responsibility of warning the people that the car pool would probably be enjoined. I knew that they had willingly suffered for nearly twelve months, but could we now ask them to walk back and forth to their jobs? And if not, would we be forced to admit that the protest had failed? For the first time I almost shrank from appearing before them.

When the evening came, I mustered sufficient courage to tell them the truth. I tried, however, to conclude on a note of hope. "We have moved all of these months," I said, "in the daring faith that God is with us in our struggle. The many experiences of days gone by have vindicated that faith in a marvelous way. Tonight we must believe that a way will be made out of no way." Yet I could feel the cold breeze of pessimism pass over the audience. The night was darker than a thousand midnights. The light of hope was about to fade and the lamp of faith to flicker.

A few hours later, before Judge Carter, the city argued that we were operating a "private enterprise" without a franchise. Our lawyers argued brilliantly that the car pool was a voluntary "share-a-ride" plan provided without profit as a service by Negro churches. It became obvious that Judge Carter would rule in favor of the city.

At noon, during a brief recess, I noticed an unusual commotion in the courtroom. Mayor Gayle was called to the back room. Several reporters moved excitedly in and out of the room. Momentarily a reporter came to the table where, as chief defendant, I sat with the lawyers. "Here is the decision that you have been waiting for," he said. "Read this release."

In anxiety and hope, I read these words: "The United States Supreme Court today unanimously ruled bus segregation unconstitutional in Montgomery, Alabama." My heart throbbed with an inexpressible joy. The darkest hour of our struggle had become the first hour of victory. Someone shouted from the back of the courtroom, "God Almighty has spoken from Washington!"

The dawn will come. Disappointment, sorrow, and despair are born at midnight, but morning follows. "Weeping may endure for a night," says the Psalmist, "but joy cometh in the morning." This faith adjourns the assemblies of hopelessness and brings new light into the dark chambers of pessimism. —Martin Luther King, Jr., *Strength To Love*

46 · "HE WHO WOULD VALIANT BE"

He who would valiant be
   'Gainst all disaster,
Let him in constancy
   Follow the Master.
There's no discouragement
   Shall make him once relent
His first avowed intent
   To be a pilgrim.

Who so beset him round
   With dismal stories,
Do but themselves confound,
   His strength the more is.
No foes shall stay his might,
   Though he with giants fight;
He will make good his right
   To be a pilgrim.

Since, Lord, thou dost defend
   Us with thy spirit,
We know we at the end
   Shall life inherit.
Then fancies flee away!

> I'll fear not what men say;
> I'll labor night and day
>   To be a pilgrim.
>
> —John Bunyan, in *The Methodist Hymnal*

47 · TO EACH HIS OWN

... Ought it, indeed, to be assumed that the lives of all men should show identical religious elements? In other words, is the existence of so many religious types and sects and creeds regrettable?

To these questions I answer "No" emphatically. And my reason is that I do not see how it is possible that creatures in such different positions and with such different powers as human individuals are, should have exactly the same functions and the same duties. No two of us have identical difficulties, nor should we be expected to work out identical solutions. Each, from his peculiar angle of observation, takes in a certain sphere of fact and trouble, which each must deal with in a unique manner. One of us must soften himself, another must harden himself; one must yield a point, another must stand firm—in order the better to defend the position assigned him. If an Emerson were forced to be a Wesley, or a Moody forced to be a Whitman, the total human consciousness of the divine would suffer. The divine can mean no single quality, it must mean a group of qualities, by being champions of which in alternation, different men may all find worthy missions. Each attitude being a syllable in human nature's total message, it takes the whole of us to spell the meaning out completely. So a "god of battles" must be allowed to be the god for one kind of person, a god of peace and heaven and home, the god for another. We must frankly recognize the fact that we live in partial systems, and that parts are not interchangeable in the spiritual like. If we are peevish and jealous, destruction of the self must be an element of our religion; why need it be one if we are good and sympathetic from the outset? If we are sick souls, we require a religion of deliverance; but why think so much of deliverance, if we are healthy-minded? Unquestionably, some men have the completer experience and the higher vocation, here just as in the social world; but for each man to stay in his own experience, whate'er it be, and for others to tolerate him there, is surely best.

—William James, *The Varieties of Religious Experience*

48 · THOUGHTS WHILE DRIVING HOME

Was I clever enough? Was I charming?
Did I make at least one good pun?
Was I disconcerting? Disarming?
Was I wise? Was I wan? Was I fun?

Did I answer that girl with white shoulders
Correctly, or should I have said
(Engagingly), "Kierkegaard smolders,
But Eliot's ashes are dead"?

And did I, while being a smarty,
Yet some wry reserve slyly keep,
So they murmured, when I'd left the party,
"He's deep. He's deep. He's deep"?

—John Updike, *Verse*

49 · HIDDEN POSSIBILITIES IN EVERY CHOICE

Out of all the possibilities, only a few can be realized. Life is a discovery of what can be developed out of the live options that face me, so constantly I make a bet on "this" rather than on "that."

Time and events move up and past, but not evenly. Some forked roads are more forked than others, some moments more packed with potency. Each situation bears hidden possibilities.

As I see my life, many things that could have happened never did, because I failed to act decisively. My life is narrower because of its *incompleted* intentions-for-good. Because of its defensive strategies. Circumstances and society made choices without me.

I realize moments of aliveness.

I was meant to be Truth. And from time to time in faith and in decision I find this truth . . . and pour myself out without reservation. I enjoy this intensity of experience in being alive. I say to myself, "This I was meant to be."

And there is *the meeting*—when I encounter someone who has discovered his truth and his integrity. This person is an *authentic* existence. He invokes my truth, for he treats me as a part of freedom. And I discover myself as a fellow participant in the risk of life and in the Kingdom of Being.

Then I crave even more to be depth and concentration of the personal. —Ross Snyder, *Inscape*

50 · SUPPLICATION AND INTERCESSION

Listen to what the apostle Paul said:
'As therefore you received Christ Jesus the Lord,

so live in him, rooted and built up on him,
and established in the faith . . .
Put on the garments that suit God's chosen people.'

Lord God our Father,
grant that as we have received Jesus Christ the Lord
so we may live in him.

That we may look upon the needs of others
   and put on the compassion of Jesus Christ:
      Father, hear our prayer
      . . . That we may live in him.

That we may put to death all arrogance and pride
   and put on the humility of Jesus Christ:
      Father, hear our prayer
      . . . That we may live in him.

That we may be set free from anger
   and put on the patience of Jesus Christ:
      Father, hear our prayer
      . . . That we may live in him.

That we may leave behind all bitterness and resentment
   and put on the forgiveness of Jesus Christ:
      Father, hear our prayer
      . . . That we may live in him.

And that in everything we do
   we may be filled with the love of Jesus Christ:
      Father, hear our prayer
      . . . That we may live in him.

To him, with you our Father, and the Holy Spirit
we give all honour and praise
now and for ever.

(Based on Colossians 2.6 RSV and 3.12-13 NEB)
—*Contemporary Prayers for Public Worship*
(Caryl Micklem, Ed.)

51 • OPEN TO THE FUTURE

... In life we need to know our goal. One of the distressing things in life is the obvious aimlessness of the lives of so many people. They are drifting anywhere instead of going somewhere. Maarten Maartens has a parable like this. "There was a man once, a satirist. In the natural course of time his friends slew him, and he died. And the people came and stood round about his corpse. 'He treated the whole round world as his football,' they said indignantly, 'and he kicked it.' The dead man opened one eye. 'But,' he said, 'always towards the goal.' " Someone once drew a cartoon showing two men on Mars looking down at the people in this world scurrying here, there and everywhere. One said to the other, "What are they doing?" The other replied, "They are going." "But," said the first, "where are they going?" "O," said the other, "they are not going anywhere; they are just going." And to go just anywhere is the certain way to arrive nowhere.

—William Barclay, *The Letters to the Corinthians*

52 • "TIME, GENTLEMEN, PLEASE"

Lie down and listen to the crabgrass grow,
The faucet leak, and learn to leave them so.
Feel how the breezes play about your hair
And sunlight settles on your breathing skin.

What else can matter but the drifting glance
On dragonfly or sudden shadow there
Of swans aloft and the whiffle of their wings
On air to other ponds? Nothing but this:
To see, to wonder, to receive, to feel
What lies in the circle of your singleness.
Think idly of a woman or a verse
Or bees or vapor trails or why the birds
Are still at noon. Yourself, be still—
There is no living when you're nagging time
And stunting every second with your will.
You work for this: to be the sovereign
Of what you slave to have—not
Slave.

—Marya Mannes, in *The Reporter*

53 · TOO MUCH VIOLENCE?

. . . We do have stupefying violence in this country [America]. It is a routine of daily life. People make money out of it; people make a science out of it; a very large number of people are entertained by it. Violence is glorified on the right and the left as the only honest and efficient political technique, and though our government issues pronunciamentos [proclamations] about the evils of violence, it has undermined its influence by using violence massively in a prolonged war in which a good part of the country does not believe.

The violence in the air today increases the likelihood that violent people, who are around in the best of times and places, will be still further inflamed. Undoubtedly, too, the murder of John Kennedy increased the likelihood of an attempt against Robert Kennedy; as he himself knew, it was bound to put thoughts into suggestible minds. . . .

Language that says too much, indignation that finds no target and spills all over the landscape raise people's tempers and add to the climate of anxiety and violence. Grieved and angered, Arthur Miller has said that we are a violent people and that the violence reflects a great deal more: "It is murderous," he said, "to tell a man he cannot live where he wishes to live." No, it is indecent, unjust, and irrational. But murder is what happened to Robert Kennedy and that is different and deserves a different feeling and invites a different analysis. When words lose their meaning, actions lose their true proportions. If everybody is so wicked, a little murder is only a little bit worse. And if everybody is implicated in a web of collective guilt, the distinction fades between one man's honest effort and another man's malingering.

—Charles Frankel, in *Saturday Review*

54 · ANYTHING FOR A LAUGH

. . . I had a sobering experience the other evening, at a preview of a film called *Villa Rides*. In the course of the picture, Charles Bronson, playing one of Villa's lieutenants, lines up three of the captured enemy "Colorados," one behind the other. He asks one of them, taller than the others, to scrunch down a bit, then steps behind them and shoots all three through the heart with a single bullet. The audience, primarily adult, howled as if it were a scene out of Laurel and Hardy!

There was more amusement, later in the film, when a commandant of General Huerta takes refuge down a well. The hiding place discovered, Bronson lights a charge of dynamite, tosses it down the well, and nonchalantly walks away. Presumably, people still laugh when, in a comedy, someone slips on a banana peel, or receives a custard pie full in the face. But *Villa Rides* is not a comedy. As written by

Robert Towne and Sam Peckinpah, it purports to be a straight and sympathetic account of Villa's efforts to sustain Madero's popular revolution of 1911. Villa, the leader of a people's army, hopes to secure liberty for all Mexicans; Huerta, the army general, wants only political advancement for himself. The film's ideological lines are drawn with at least some regard for historic fact; its people and places are real.

But this is merely the nut within the shell, and pitifully little nutriment it offers. For it quickly becomes evident that the film's historicity is merely a pretext, an excuse to douse the screen with one bloodbath after another. The Colorados sweep into a small town and proceed to rape, murder, and hang the inhabitants (the latter act shown in particularly grisly detail). Whereupon Villa's irregulars swarm in and, in glorious Technicolor, decimate the soldiery; their officers are penned up and shot in small batches as they attempt to escape. A Villa henchman is deterred from making unwelcome advances to a woman by a bullet in the stomach, then told to go outside to die. A trainload of Colorados is ambushed, then blown to pieces as Bronson and Robert Mitchum fly over it in a small plane, pelting it with homemade bombs that they nonchalantly light with their cigars.

What makes this all so horrifying is not the sheer number of corpses, nor even the cold-blooded, gruesome devices by which they are produced, although to be sure these have their own high quotient of horror. But more profoundly disturbing is the film-makers' obvious and implicit belief that their sadistic catalogue of gory death can be turned out in today's market in the name of entertainment. . . .

—Arthur Knight, in *Saturday Review*

55 · COMMENTS ON PHILIPPIANS 4:8-9

. . . The word **think** is translated as equivalent to "calculate," i.e., one is not simply to think about **these things,** but to think about them as though he were calculating the cost of committing himself to them in action. Commentators have often suggested that this list of abstract virtues and principles which reason should ponder is an indication of Greek influence upon the apostle. A final judgment cannot be made on such issues, but it is important to connect this paragraph with the whole Christian position that moral or spiritual truth with which Christianity is concerned *must* be expressed in living persons. It cannot be abstracted from action, put into words like purity, honor, loveliness, excellence, and have power to move the will to action. All **these things** to which Paul refers are qualities of life known only when lived by persons. Such an interpretation is confirmed in the sentence that follows, where Paul says: **what you have . . . seen in me, do.**

—Robert F. Wicks, in *The Interpreter's Bible*

56 · "THE RELIGIOUS DIMENSION AND THE IDEA OF GOD"

. . . The religious dimension [of experience] involves viewing our life and experience as having a ground and a final purpose. The possibility of such a ground and a purpose first becomes explicit through experience of the crisis events [i.e., being born, attaining puberty, choosing a vocation, getting married, giving birth, dying] and their disclosure of the holy depth of life. These experiences are occasions upon which man's capacity as a religious animal is realized, for at the crucial turning points in human life man becomes aware of actually attending to and wondering about his own being, about the mystery that, though he individually might not have been, he nevertheless is. At such times he is led to ponder the purpose of existence as such. The crucial times, moreover, force an awareness that man is a dependent being, that he is not self-sustaining, and that he needs to find an object of supreme worth to which he can devote himself if he is to achieve self-realization. This threefold awareness to which we are led represents, from the side of purely human experience, the material of the religious dimension. The events of crisis do not themselves constitute any resolution of the religious question, but merely provide the *occasions* upon which man discovers the meaning of the religious question and the urgency of his need for an answer. It is an error to suppose that the religious dimension of experience is itself positive religious faith, or that it is the "material" out of which the reality of God is, so to speak, constructed. To think in these terms would be to think of experience as somehow constituting reality instead of being a medium through which reality is disclosed.

There is, however, an essential connection between the religious dimension with its cycle of crucial events and the idea of God. The connection becomes manifest at the point where the sense of awe in the presence of the holy ground of life disclosed in the special occasions of life is grasped as concentrated in one supreme reality and identified with God. There is an asymmetry in the order of events. From a purely logical standpoint we cannot pass from the experience of awe and power to the God who is disclosed in and through the special revelatory events that define the substance of Christian faith. The order must be reversed; the idea of the God in whom Christians believe must first be presupposed in order for the identification to take place. And indeed it is possible for a person to be overcome with a sense of awe and to raise the question of the ground and purpose of existence on these occasions without at the same time believing that the Christian God is present at all. But it does not follow that the crucial times at which the religious dimension of experience becomes explicit contribute nothing to an understanding of the idea of God. If belief in God in the religious sense is to make a difference in the conduct of life on the level of the profane [i.e., everyday, commonplace experiences], the meaning of that belief must be related to human experience in all of its dimension. The reality of God from the religious standpoint means the answering of the question about the ground and purpose of human life. Failure to understand this point is a major factor in the perpetuation of merely conventional religion in which belief in God is either the fulfillment of a duty imposed by an institution or the inert belief that, in addition to all the finite things that exist, there is one more existent being called "God." If, however, the religious dimension of experience is understood and taken seriously, belief in God takes on new meaning. Belief in God then means belief in a reality of whose presence we are especially aware on the crucial occasions of life and it means a reality upon whom we depend for our being, our purpose, and our fulfillment.

—John E. Smith, *Experience and God*

57 · A REAL FIGHT

... He [Paul] insists to those Corinthians who wanted to take the easy way of things that no man will ever get anywhere without the sternest self-discipline. Paul was always fascinated by the picture of the athlete. An athlete must train with intensity if he is to win his contest; and Corinth knew how thrilling contests could be, for at Corinth the Isthmian games, which were second only to the Olympic games were held. Furthermore, these athletes undergo this self-discipline and this training to win a crown of laurel leaves that within days will be a withered chaplet. How much more should the

Christian discipline himself to win the crown which is eternal life?

. . . .

... To win this fight and to be victorious in this race demands discipline. We have to discipline our bodies; it is one of the neglected facts of the spiritual life that very often spiritual depression springs from nothing else than physical unfitness. If a man is going to do his best work in anything he must bring to it a body as fit as he can make it. We neglect our physical health at our peril. We have to discipline our minds; it is one of the tragedies of life that men refuse to think until they are incapable of thinking. We can never solve problems by refusing to see them or by running away from them. We must discipline our souls; we can do so by facing life's sorrows with calm endurance; life's temptations with all the strength that we can bring to them in the strength of God; life's disappointments with courage. There is not a day when life does not bring us opportunities to discipline our souls. —William Barclay, *The Letters to the Corinthians*

58 · "I WANT A PRINCIPLE WITHIN"

I want a principle within
  Of watchful, godly fear,
A sensibility of sin,
  A pain to feel it near.
Help me the first approach to feel
  Of pride or wrong desire,
To catch the wandering of my will,
  And quench the kindling fire.

If to the right or left I stray,
  That moment, Lord, reprove,

And let me weep my life away
  For having grieved thy love.
Give me to feel an idle thought
  As actual wickedness,
And mourn for the minutest fault
  In exquisite distress.

From thee that I no more may stray,
  No more thy goodness grieve,
Grant me the filial awe, I pray,
  The tender conscience give;
Quick as the apple of an eye,
  O God, my conscience make!
Awake my soul when sin is nigh,
  And keep it still awake.

Almighty God of truth and love,
  To me thy power impart;
The burden from my soul remove,
  The hardness from my heart.
O may the least omission pain
  My reawakened soul,
And drive me to that grace again,
  Which makes the wounded whole.
—Charles Wesley, in *The Methodist Hymnal*

59 · EXPRESSING CONVICTIONS

[Many Christians today believe the technicalities of the faith should be, and always have been, left to the professional theologian. This was not the case in the early church. Here is a description of the church in the East in the late fourth century.]

The whole city is full of it, the squares, the market places, the cross-roads, the alleyways; old-clothes men, money changers, food sellers: they are all busy arguing. If you ask someone to give you change, he philosophizes about the Begotten and the Unbegotten; if you inquire about the price of a loaf, you are told by way of reply that the Father is greater and the Son inferior; if you ask 'Is my bath ready?' the attendant answers that the Son was made out of nothing. . . . —Timothy Ware, *The Orthodox Church*

60 · THE NECESSITY OF COMMITMENT

It is generally recognized that though commitment is of the first importance, men may have more than one object of their commitment. The full commitment of millions of Germans, prior to and during the Great War, was to Adolf Hitler and *his* cause. Other millions are today committed to Marxism. This is why it is now recognized that Marxian communism is fundamentally a religion rather than a mere economic or political system. The fact that it denies God does not keep it from being religious. Christians have no monopoly on commitment; they simply have a different object. A Christian is a person who confesses that, amidst the manifold and confusing voices heard in the world, there is one Voice which supremely wins his full assent, uniting all his powers, intellectual and emotional, into a single pattern of self-giving. That Voice is Jesus Christ. A Christian not only believes *that* He was; he believes *in Him* with all his heart and strength and mind. Christ appears to the Christian as the one stable point or fulcrum in all the relativities of history. Once the Christian has made this primary commitment he still has perplexities, but he begins to know the joy of being used for a mighty purpose, by which his little life is dignified.

—Elton Trueblood, *The Company of the Committed*

61 · REVELATION

I used to wonder
  why God had trouble
  with revelation.
Why couldn't he
  make himself known
  with such dramatic power
  that none could disbelieve?

Then one day
  I tried it.

An agnostic
  strained to see me
  through the thick filter
  of his doubt,
  but he could not.
Over and over
  he said,
  "Prove that you have worth:
  then I will believe."
But I knew he would not—
  even if I turned stones to bread,
  walked on water,
  and rose from the dead.

I was trapped
  by doubt,
And could reveal
  no more of myself
  than another was willing to accept.

Then I knew
  why God had trouble
  with revelation.

      —William T. Joyner, *Wheels in the Air*

62 · DOUBT AND DESPAIR

[Harry Emerson Fosdick recounts his early days in his study for the ministry. He raced frantically toward what could have become a mental collapse. The crisis arose not from trouble but from exhilarating happiness. Opportunity was driving him almost beyond sanity.]

Many times . . . I have faced people who started in to tell me the inner hell of their neurotic agony—the waves of melancholia, the obsessive anxieties, the desire for suicide and all the rest—and I have stopped them, saying: "Don't you tell me, let me tell you how you feel." One typical man, with wide eyes, exclaimed when I was through: "My God! how did you know that?"

In one of my later sermons I note a passage telling how young Tolstoi, utterly disheartened, decided to kill himself; how Mark Twain, thirty years old, put a loaded pistol to his head but lacked the courage to pull the trigger; how William James, who inspired my generation as few men did, in his dispirited youth almost committed suicide. My congregation at Riverside did not recognize, I am sure, that those references were autobiographical. One dreadful day I reached the pit of utter despair, sure that all my hopes were vain and that I was finished. I have often wondered whether, if my father had not been there saying, "Harry! Harry!" I would really have cut my throat with that razor.

. . . .

This whole horrid experience was one of the most important factors in my preparation for the ministry. For the first time in my life, I faced, at my wit's end, a situation too much for me to handle. I went down into the depths where self-confidence becomes ludicrous. There the technique I had habitually relied upon—marshaling my wit and my volition and going strenuously after what I wanted—petered completely out. The harder I struggled, the worse I was. It was what I did the struggling with that was sick. I, who had thought myself strong, found myself beaten, unable to cope not only with outward circumstances but even with myself. In that experience I learned some things about religion that theological seminaries do not teach. I learned to pray, not because I had adequately argued out prayer's rationality, but because I desperately needed help from a Power greater than my own. I learned that God, much more than a theological proposition, is an immediately available Resource; that just as around our bodies is a physical universe from which we draw all our physical energy, so around our spirits is a spiritual Presence in living communion with whom we can find sustaining strength. . . .

—Harry Emerson Fosdick, *The Living of These Days*

63 · THE CRISIS OF DOUBT

Doubt only risks being offensive when it is directed against ideas and attitudes which are fondly cherished. The fondest ideas are the ideas from which we derive our sense of support in life. When these are attacked, doubting ceases to be a game and becomes a battle. But the doubting side of our mind knows we ought not surrender to inadequate ideas and attitudes. So it presses its weight against the ideas to see if they will really hold. This function of doubt is especially relevant considering how habitual our ideas and attitudes tend to become. Were it not for doubt's tireless cross-examination, we would find the inertia of our attitudes carrying us beyond the time of their usefulness. Doubt warns us when the vehicle we are driving is no longer up to the demands of modern transportation. We need not have our breakdown on the road. . . .

THE INNER LIFE

Ideas and beliefs have what Ortega y Gasset [a Spanish philosopher] has called an orthopaedic character. They are always subject to fracture. It is the business of doubt to warn us before the load of life breaks them and leaves us in crisis.
—Carl Michalson, *Faith for Personal Crises*

64 ·

"*All right, so your hair is coming down a little bit. . . . If you were deeply spiritual, you wouldn't worry so much about outward appearances!*"
—Charles M. Schulz, *What Was Bugging Ol' Pharaoh?*

65 · HOLD TO CHRIST

"We need a return," said a writer in *The Times* (January 5, 1963), "not so much to 'Christianity'—that complex of doctrines, organizations, liturgies, traditions and even social habits, which would always be partly a man-made thing—as to faith in, and personal commitment to Christ Himself as the Lord of all life, the revealer both of man's meaning for God and of God's meaning for man."

Once such a commitment has been made, a wide margin of agnosticism [i.e., doubt about specifically "Christian" doctrines] is, in my view, permissible. "Hold to Christ," said Professor Butterfield, Vice-Chancellor of Cambridge University, and a Methodist lay preacher, "and for the rest be totally uncommitted." I feel that, once such a commitment is made, one cannot go back on it finally, any more than a faithful husband, having established a love relationship with his wife, can go back on her, though she may often puzzle him and set up doubt and even irritation in regard to less important matters. Doubt, and the mental wrestling it engenders, are surely the way to a deeper and better grounded faith than is possible to those who can, with naïve facility, accept what is told them. "It is not like a child that I believe in Christ and confess Him," said Dostoevsky when he was criticized for the reactionary character of his faith. *"My hosanna has come forth from the crucible of doubt."* In my own little way, I feel the same.   —Leslie D. Weatherhead, *The Christian Agnostic*

66 · MY FATE

A writer has said that a person's character is marked not so much by what life does to him as to the reaction he makes to life's circumstance.

Yes, but I have been handicapped through no fault of my own. A physical disability is nothing to pass by simply. Whether I like it or not, I am limited in certain activities because of that disability. More, I have not had the opportunities of leisurely living that come to those with financial stability. Hence, I could not take time to read, to study, to travel, to cultivate the beginnings of artistic ability, which leisure permits. I have had to be busy with mundane pursuits, just to exist!

Yet, come to think about it, my reaction to these things is the important fact! Either I could bewail my fate, such a pleasant thing to do to excuse my lack of gumption, and thus place the blame on life itself; or I could take my life up into my hands and make of it what it could be under the circumstances. After all, it is in my power, and in no one else's power, what I do with my life.

—Harold Wiley Freer and Francis B. Hall,
Two or Three Together

67 · PRAYER LIFE IN A GROUP

A story is told of an intercessory prayer cell in a large city, made up of hardworking women who found themselves often too tired to welcome the thought of another meeting. Each time before one woman went she would say to her husband, "I just can't go out again tonight," but she always went; and every time she would come home all aglow with the joy of the glorious fellowship that she had experienced. It was one of this group, a harried little laundress, who said, "Here inside of me I have a quiet no man can take from me." The group lighted one another; they prayed for irate cooks as well as for Stalin with an equal fervor and good will. Love and joy and peace are a contagion. The Holy Spirit stirs in the heart of a member and one by one each is kindled to release healing energies into the world.

. . . .

Fellowships of the concerned inevitably have miracles in their midst. A person who has had years of healing experience says that two requirements are essential: first, faith that opens the door to God's power and peace; second, a caring love that opens the door of the suffering brother or sister to receive this peace. These bring about the miracles of healing, body, mind and soul.

—Harold Wiley Freer and Francis B. Hall,
Two or Three Together

68 · HAZARDS WITHIN SMALL GROUP LIFE

An undue pride in the grandeur of the building [sanctuary] is by no means the only danger which arises when a single aspect of Christianity is emphasized disproportionately. Another equal but different danger arises from the nurture of the small prayer group. While there can be no doubt that the rediscovery of the power of the small group has been one of the genuine Christian advances in our generation, it is possible that the prayer group, like the sanctuary, *may* involve a retreat from reality. A prayer group is dangerous, and even harmful, if the members are satisfied to indulge in their own delightful fellowship, making this fellowship essentially an end in itself. The society of a little group of fellow believers can be so pleasant that the poverty and the sorrow of the outside world are forgotten, at least for the time of meeting. But the poverty and the sorrow must never be forgotten, not even for a little while. A prayer group which does not make its members more effective apostles in their jobs and homes, and more sensitive participators in the fellowship of those who bear the mark of frustration, is essentially a failure. The test of the vitality of a group does not occur primarily while the group is meeting; it occurs after the meeting is over.

—Elton Trueblood, *The Company of the Committed*

69 · ARE WE LIVING OUR FAITH?

. . . Jesus said that the way we reveal our love for God found in quiet is through love for man in daily life. For Him the test of our faith is what we do about it in daily living.

1. Criticism of others disappears. Our critical attitude of tearing apart our friends and enemies, of objecting to their inefficiencies or their weaknesses, of asking how "they get that way," suddenly disappears. We not only find that we have lost this common trait, but hearing folk attack others critically disturbs us.

2. Everyone seems so friendly. Beneath the worry and anxiety of our living we sense the open faces and smiling hearts of people. Our smiles in return bring a warmth and a joy that fill our whole being.

3. We reach out with love to all we meet, even the strangers we have not seen before. We want to help everyone, to make certain they too are happy. Just ordinary kindnesses begin to multiply, and we find that normal courtesies and thoughtful deeds are part of everyday living. We have no desire to help only those who can help us; we just want to help folk, any folk, who need what we have or can offer.

4. We seek little common tasks in church and community. These once seemed so puny, things hardly worth our time. Now we want to help make drapes, to work at a supper,

to teach a class, to do some typing, to clean a room, to paint a chair, to visit in a shutin's home. Just to be doing something for the church or community is really doing something for God—how joyous is that feeling!

5. Our money begins to assume new significance. We need less and less for ourselves, and we want to give more and more for others. We lose interest in extra clothing and extra desserts and midday snacks and luxuries that we thought quite necessary. We seek ways of saving from our regular allowances, as well as cutting down on our regular expenditures, that we may have gifts to share with others.

6. We rearrange our time. We spend less time in beauty parlors, in movies, in other forms of commercial recreation, in seeking pleasure for ourselves alone. We begin to drop out of some organizations and committees through which we have been scattering our energies, that we may give more time to fewer things, yet truly give enough time to these to make our work effective. We begin putting first things first, surprising ourselves by the amount of time we have and the amount of work we now can do. In office and in home and in school we are amazed as we wonder why we never had worked out such a fine time schedule before.

7. We find that our minds reach out far beyond their former horizons. We no longer are provincial, thinking of self, of immediate family, of immediate neighborhood. We seek books, friends, classes, entertainment that will enlarge our minds and our thinking. We begin to read and talk and think about social problems, about race and industry and government. Good housing and juvenile delinquency and correct voting and care for the needy and the general welfare of those in any need begin to be part of our living. . . .

—Harold Wiley Freer and Francis B. Hall,
Two or Three Together

70 · IN THE HOLY SPIRIT

. . . We pray to you, Spirit of God, creator,
complete the work you have begun,
prevent the evil we are capable of doing
and inspire us toward what is good—
to faithfulness and patience,
to compassion and gentleness,
and waken in us friendship
for every living being
and with joy for everything
that is good and human. . . .
You are our will to live,
the love that keeps us here on earth
and ties us to our God.
You urge us on to go on to the end
and to endure everything,
not to give way and to go on hoping,
as love does.
You are the soul of all our prayers
so there is nothing we may not expect from you—
wisdom to understand each other,
readiness to help each other
and everything we need.
If you are God's gift to us.
Be present here among us, then,
God in us.

—Huub Oosterhuis, *Your Word Is Near*

CHAPTER 7—OUR FEELINGS AND OUR FAITH

71 · CHANGING WORLD OF VALUES

James Bond, whom we have taken as a reflection of a changing world of values, fills his leisure hours with fun time. He is one of the new breed of pleasure seekers—not that pleasure is a new pursuit, but the means of pursuit are far more ingenious today. Bond loves to gamble for big stakes, and his expense-account job enables him to jump from continent to continent, casino to casino. Baccarat seems to be his favorite game, but he is equally adept at cards, golf, and scissors-cut-paper. On all of them he is willing to gamble a wallet and cheat to win. Mr. Bond is also a drinking man who is willing to take on any bottle from rotgut to the bonded best. He's fond of sports cars, proud of his racing change, and willing to consider every driver on the road his competitor. At other times you might think Bond's god is his belly, for he loves to eat and is very particular about what and where he eats.

James Bond's fun time is devoted to gambling, guzzling, gunning, gourmandism. These pleasure pursuits are no longer just the sports of kings, wealthy playboys, and the jet set. They are within the reach of many. With the increase of affluence and leisure, John Doe can blow a little, and possibly a lot, of his ready cash on Saturday night poker or a weekend in Las Vegas. He can stock his own liquor cabinet and join the cocktail set. He can buy a little sports car and drag off for the rally. Credit cards have made great fun out of restaurant hopping. Feed now and finance later. The beaches are crowded, the lakes are crammed. Culture and cookouts are big business.

This is great, and many of us need a fun break. Fun, in its proper perspective, we all need! But there are signs of a new hedonism, the pursuit of pleasure as an end in itself, as the chief measure of man's meaning. If pleasure becomes the *summum bonum,* the highest good, the pursuit of happiness may get out of hand. "Can we survive the fun explosion?" . . .

—Lycurgus M. Starkey, Jr., *James Bond's World of Values*

72 · RELIGION AS FEELING

... When religion was preached as feeling, the male section of the German congregations stopped going to church. When they were told that religion is not a matter of clear knowledge and moral action, but of feeling, they reacted. I can tell you this from my own participation in the nineteenth-century situation. The churches became empty. Neither the youth nor the men were satisfied with feeling. They looked for sharp thought and moral significance in the sermons. When religion was reduced to feeling and weakened by sentimental hymns—instead of the great old hymns which had religious power of the presence of the divine—people lost interest in the churches.

Schleiermacher's concept of religion as feeling [of absolute dependence on God] had unfortunate consequences in this country too. When I discuss theology with antitheological colleagues, they are very happy if they can quote somebody who puts religion into a dark corner of mere subjective feeling. Religion is not dangerous there. They can use their scientific and political words, their ethical and logical analysis, etc., without regard to religion, and the churches can be removed to one side. They do not have to be taken very seriously for they deal with the realm of subjective feelings. We do not participate in such things, but if there are people who do have such desires, let them go to church. We do not mind. But in the moment in which they are confronted by a theology which interferes very much—not from the outside but from the inside—with the scientific process, political movements, and moral principles, and which wants to show that within all of them there is an ultimate concern, as I call it, or an unconditional dependence, as Schleiermacher called it, then these people react. Then they want to put religion back into the realm of feeling. And if theology itself,

or religion itself, allows them to do this, they are doing a disservice. Such a preaching of religious feeling does a great disservice to religion. —Paul Tillich
Perspectives on 19th and 20th Century Protestant Theology

73 · EMOTION IN RELIGION

... Question: Granted that by feeling Schleiermacher did not mean subjective emotion, nevertheless, his *Speeches* are not unemotional in character, and having emotion is an undeniable part of being human. What is the role of the emotions in the religious life for you and Schleiermacher?

Answer: ... Nobody can exclude the element of feeling in any experience in which the total personality is involved, and in religion this is perhaps more true than in any other realm. It is certainly true that the response of our whole being in immediacy—which might be the right definition of feeling—can be seen in an earnest prayer or in the worship service of a community, or in listening to the prophetic word. This emotional element is there. Let us take an example from the arts. You are deeply grasped by a painting at which you are looking while visiting an art gallery; you are taken into it; you live in it and your emotions are strongly awakened. But if someone should say that your aesthetic experience is only emotion, you would answer that it is more than that. If it were only emotion, it would not have this definite character which is given through this kind of painting. I recognize, in this moment in which I am emotionally moved, a dimension of reality which otherwise I would never be aware, and a dimension in myself would never be opened up except through participation in the painting.

I would say the same thing about music. Music is often said to be completely in the realm of feeling. This is true, but it is a very special kind of feeling which is related to the particular musical figures and forms which make music a work of art. This also reveals to you a dimension of being, including your being, which would otherwise not be revealed if there were no musical impact on you. So we can say that although the emotional element is always present in experience of whatever kind, you cannot say that a certain experience is only emotion. Take the experience of love. You cannot say that love is emotion. Love has an element of emotion in it and very much so, but it is not an emotion. It is a reunion, as I would call it, of separated entities that belong to each other eternally. This experience cannot be identified with the personal reaction which we call feeling.

—Paul Tillich
Perspectives on 19th and 20th Century Protestant Theology

74 · A PRAYER?

O Lord, so long as the weather is reasonably fine,
  so long as I have no visitors,
  so long as nobody asks me to do any work,
  so long as I can sit in the back pew but one on
    the left,
  so long as it isn't a local preacher planned,
  so long as they don't choose hymns I don't know,
  so long as my Joe is asked to recite at the
    Anniversary,
  so long as I can get home in time for the play,
I will honour Thee with my presence at Church whenever I feel like it.

—David Head, *He Sent Leanness*

75 · PLEASURE AND MEANING

... The work of all of us, whether it be scientific, technical, commercial, educational, artistic, industrial, argicultural, or manual, has its appointed place in the divine adventure of the world. We all play our part in the adventure. We all share in the divine joy of adventure; the joy of doing something useful which has a meaning in the total purpose of the world; the joy of bringing forth fruit. That is the image which Jesus himself often used in order to express the meaning of human life (John 15:5). Life is the current, the sap that flows into us day by day from God. Our work, all we do, feel, think, and believe—these are the fruits which it ripens in us.

That is why faith, far from turning us away from the world, brings us back to it. That is why it awakens in us a new interest in the world, in the concrete reality of everyday, hard, laborious, difficult, often painful as it is, but wonderful nevertheless. The joy of living, of making an effort, of having a goal to aim at; the joy of moving a finger, of smelling a perfume, of looking at something, of hearing a voice, of learning something and loving someone. The pleasure of research, of success, of study; the pleasure of discovery, or rather of the hope of discovery, of the excitement of wrestling with a difficult problem; the pleasure of understanding something one did not understand before, of knowing what one did not know; the pleasure of the puzzle and its solution.
—Paul Tournier, *The Adventure of Living*

76 · FEELING AND TRAGEDY

[This letter and many others by the sister-in-law of the late Dietrich Bonhoeffer, the German martyr, were written to a friend in Ohio. The letters relate eye-witness accounts of the Auschwitz trials.]

A large number of women with small children are told to strip before the so-called "shower rooms"; one mother, carrying a maybe one-year-old, until now gullible enough that she simply could not let herself believe the rumors that circulated about the camp, suddenly sees what is to happen. Gripped by despair, she throws herself down at the feet of a young guard imploring him to save at least her child. And she reminds him that he surely has wife and child himself and that he therefore must have mercy. What shall he do? He pushes her aside and shoves her forward with the others, across the threshold and inside. But at the moment when the doors are closing, screaming My Wife! My Child! he thrusts himself into the throng, and dies with them there in the gas.

—Emmi Bonhoeffer
Auschwitz Trials: Letters from an Eyewitness

77 · A CONSTRUCTIVE ROLE

Many people have a ... negative conception of Christianity, as if it consisted in continual self-amputation, as if God wanted to hold us down, rather than that we should 'turn again and live.' Would such a God deserve the name of Father which Christ gave to him? When I labour to liberate a crushed life, I am not fighting against God, but with him. Like a gardener who removes from around a plant the weeds that choke it, using all the care that as one of God's creatures it deserves, I am helping to re-establish his purpose of life.

It is God who gave it life, and he surely wants it to flourish and bear fruit. Does not Christ often speak of bearing fruit? Bearing fruit means being oneself, asserting oneself, growing in accordance with God's purpose.

Christianity, therefore, has its positive, affirmative, creative aspect—ignored by many Christians. I do not deny that it imposes certain specific acts of renunciation. Jesus spoke of the husbandman who prunes his vine so that it may bear more fruit. The purpose of pruning is not to restrict life, but on the contrary to promote its fuller and richer flow.

Christian life, then, is liberty, the liberation of the person from the trammels imposed by external influences. It is the rising of the sap from within. It is life under God's leadership. It is a balance between prayer and action: between the dialogue in which his creative inspiration is sought, and the bold and confident affirmation of self, in which the inspiration received is put into practice. . . .
—Paul Tournier, *The Meaning of Persons*

78 · TO LIVE IS TO CHOOSE

. . . There is less faith put in reason as a guide for humanity today than was the case in the last century. The atomic bomb has something to do with this. Those scientists who are in the van of scientific progress are themselves afraid of the dangers inherent in it. After having made a public apology to the Japanese people, Professor Robert Moon, one of the nuclear physicists who helped to create the atomic bomb, declared to the Moral Rearmament assembly that this mortal danger would only be removed if we began to listen to what God was saying to us: 'In our time,' he added, 'the Holy Spirit must take first place, and the intellect must come second.'

In any case, this gigantic effort to rediscover the great laws of life by means of rational judgment must lead to the turning of them into a rigid morality, a system of abstract principles, like all moralistic systems crushing in its effect. It is not living, but cold and dead. And sooner or later one sees that, in spite of the sincerest of resolves, true fidelity to such principles is impossible. Then there is nothing left but despair or the philosophy of compromises, unless another solution is found, in living fellowship with God: the experience of forgiveness.

It is characteristic of Christianity that choice is made not of principles but of a person, of the living God, of Christ. It does indeed bring with it all the moral principles that can be discovered by reason. But it makes us something more than mere machines applying principles: it makes us persons. It brings us much more than a code of ethics. It brings us a personal relationship, a current of life springing from the very source of all life, and true liberty.

—Paul Tournier, *The Meaning of Persons*

79 · PERPLEXED, BUT NOT UNTO DESPAIR

... It seems that suffering would rule out the quality of joy from the Christian life. But, paradoxically, it is in the most intense moments of existential pain that the power of God's presence gives rise to joy. In this case joy is not the opposite of sorrow or of suffering but the "yes-saying" to life within the combination of pleasure and pain made possible by the assurance that the powers of the future age are those which sustain, purify, and establish the present act of love. Hence, even in the presence of death or of tragedy, one is basically joyful, because the meaning of his life is fulfilled by love, not by success or continued existence.

It is easy to cheapen joy by identifying it with "happiness" or absence of pain. Christian joy, however, is always in context with courageous decision and suffering love. Joy suggests a quality of the being of a Christian, the set of his orientation in existence. It is the direct accompaniment of one's acceptance and living within God's "yes" to man in Jesus Christ. The good news, the gospel of the New Testament, consists not in announcing a life free of difficulty and suffering, but

in the announcement of the presence of God to renew, to restore, to redeem the meaning of life within the polarities of pain and pleasure, of suffering and happiness. . . .
The experience of God's grace becomes formative for the Christian's interpretation of the life of all men. Hence, by anticipation, by hope, he draws all existence into the future of God's action, imparting to all the love and the grace of the fragmentary experience, the reversal of the achievement orientation. . . . There are persons with real joy who are not Christians. But there are no Christians without joy.
—Jack Boozer and William A. Beardslee, *Faith to Act*

80 · J. B.

[J. B., modern counterpart to Job, and Sarah, wife of J. B., have been informed of the tragic death of their last child.]

. . . Sarah: David . . . Jonathan . . . Mary . . . Ruth . . .

J. B.:   Sarah!

Silence.

   Listen to me!

Silence.

   Sarah!
Even desperate we can't despair—
Let go each other's fingers—sink
Numb in that dumb silence—drown there
Sole in our cold selves . . .

> We cannot! . . .
>
> God is there too, in the desperation.
> I do not know why God should strike
> But God is what is stricken also:
> Life is what despairs in death
> And, desperate, is life still . . .
>
> > Sarah!
>
> Do not let my hand go, Sarah!
>
> Say it after me:
>
> > The Lord
>
> Giveth . . . Say it.

Sarah: *mechanically*   The Lord giveth.

J. B.:   The Lord taketh away . . .

Sarah: *flinging his hand from hers, shrieking*
> Takes!
>
> Kills! Kills! Kills! Kills!

Silence.

J. B.:   Blessed be the name of the Lord.

The light fades.

—Archibald MacLeish, *J. B.*

81 · REVELATION

... Revelation is the communication of God's secrets by God himself. We would never know anything for sure about him, his mercy, his intention, his work, his plan, if he had not said it himself. What distinguishes him from the impassive God of philosophers is that he did not remain all alone, that he chose for himself a partner "in his image," with whom he can enter into conversation. And it is always he who speaks first; everything begins with the Word of God, that of man is never anything but a response.

Moreover it is not only to mankind in general or to the great prophets that he speaks. He speaks to each of us; he is personally interested in every one of us; he speaks personally to each of us and he listens to each of us personally, and that is what completes the process of making a person of us. The person, in the full sense of the word, is man in personal relationship, not only with others, but with God.

Hence, . . . the formation of a person. Man remains more or less a child, unconscious, irresponsible, an automaton activated by his instincts and reflexes, so long as he has not had the personal encounter with God, so long as he has not accepted the difficult dialogue with God. The first stage in the formation of a person was a withdrawal, becoming an individual by the creation of a personal secret. The second stage was the free communication of this secret to someone else freely chosen, and out of it the experience of love and the interpersonal relationship with another. And the third stage is to have this double experience in our relations with God, to feel ourselves distinct from him, to choose him also freely, to tell him our secret and to know thereby the interpersonal relationship with him, the experience of the love of God. . . .

—Paul Tournier, *Secrets*

82 · THE MOST IMPORTANT QUESTION

QUESTION: What do you consider the most important question of our time?

ANSWER: This country [America] is proud of its standard of living, its democratic freedom, its civilizing goods, and above all its technological skills. I consider it a question of fundamental import—a question which will have real political consequences—whether we men of today learn to distinguish between what makes our existence pleasanter *and* easier and what it was created to be, what can be called its real theme.

All these civilizing goods—from television to supermarkets—are merely means which smooth our path through the world and make it easier to travel. But what will it profit us, if we make smooth social and technical progress on this level road and no longer know *where* we are going, in whose *name* we are living, and what the *goal* of our destiny is? For then perfectionism in the way in which we master life leads precisely to a life which has not been mastered. Then we shall be wandering aimlessly over a smooth and level plain.

May it not be that our neuroses and our predilection for psychiatrists derive from the fact that we have become a heap of misery in this great empty plain? What good are our refrigerators, what good is the well–oiled apparatus of our style of living, if we no longer know what we are living for?

Albert Einstein once said that we live in an age of perfect means and confused ends. The question which is inherent in that statement I consider to be the most important question of our times. It has to do with the boredom which is deadly, with the emptiness which frightens us, but also with the fulfillments which make life worth living. It has to do with the crucial task which has been set for us, namely, to distinguish between the "means," which make our life *easier,* and the "meaning" of our life, which is the only thing that makes life *possible*. Even the person who has perfectly solved the problem of the means can still perish in suicide because a life without meaning is dreadful. And this dreadfulness actually increases as the outward course of this life grows smoother.

I can express what I mean by this as a Christian in the words of our Lord: "What will it profit a man, if he gains the whole world and forfeits his life?" All the means of mastering the world can turn a man into a fool if he overlooks the crucial question. That this should *not* happen, I consider the most important question of our time.

—Helmut Thielicke, *Between Heaven and Earth*

83 · LONELINESS

... A stone, a leaf, an unfound door; of a stone, a leaf, a door. And of all the forgotten faces.

Naked and alone we came into exile. In her dark womb we did not know our mother's face; from the prison of her flesh have we come into the unspeakable and incommunicable prison of this earth.

Which of us has known his brother? Which of us has looked into his father's heart? Which of us has not remained forever prison-pent? Which of us is not forever a stranger and alone?

O waste of loss, in the hot mazes, lost, among bright stars on this most weary unbright cinder, lost! Remembering speechlessly we seek the great forgotten language, the lost lane-end into heaven, a stone, a leaf, an unfound door. Where? When?

O lost, and by the wind grieved, ghost, come back again.

—Thomas Wolfe, *Look Homeward Angel*

84 · SEEKING TO BELONG

... The search for community among young people today is based on the deepest part of man's awareness—his compassion, his self-understanding, even his suffering. It is this, above anything else, that puts the young today beyond rebellion, that means they are not simply fighting the old standards but establishing new ones, that even means they are not simply "copping out," which is negative, but are "dropping out," which can be positive when it implies an attempt to find something to drop back into. Where the genuine attempt to establish community prevails over more temporary attitudes and activities, there, I think, our young people have something to offer American society.

And what can the middle-class, middle-aged square do about it, anyway? We (for I include myself among that group) can begin by trying to understand that nothing a human being is or does can be understood apart from the most basic human motives and needs and that the most important things about hippies and draft-card burners and tough community organizers in the inner city are not their differences from the rest of us but their similarities. Next, we can learn to listen to them, because they are not really fighting us; nobody in search for community is really looking for a fight. Nor do they want to exclude us. If they are looking at the deepest level for some meaning in life, they are looking at a level at which any man can participate. And finally, we can look again at our own institutions to see where the radical criticism of these institutions implied by the young people of this study really has relevance.

Suppose, for example, that the churches again became resorts for community, where people could become radical in the sense of getting at the real root of things with honesty and mutual acceptance, where real love flourished. Suppose, to

put it more concretely, the church were a place where hippies and teeny-boppers, political radicals, some Harlem heroin addicts, and a sprinkling of middle-class straights could all talk out their feelings and desires, in perfect, loving honesty, and all would feel accepted. If that would happen, even the church would have returned to what it once was. That is the sort of thing that many young people today are implicity offering us.
—Delbert L. Earisman, *Hippies in Our Midst*

85 · THOSE WE BEFRIEND

. . . The Indians have an interesting thought that it is always a privilege to help a Brahman [a Hindu of the highest caste], even a Brahman beggar, because you are helping a man in whom God dwells more fully than in any other caste. Jesus, it seems to me, would teach, as a similar thought, that it is always a privilege to help anybody, because all men are of the same caste, the very highest caste. They are all sons of God. They are men in whom God dwells. And, indeed, I think it is not poetic fancy merely, but the naked truth. That by coming to men with nothing but a loving desire to help them you do actually come near to God Himself; perhaps nearer than when you kneel before the altar. And if I were asked to prove that point I should say that the proof lies in the fact that you cannot render disinterested service without feeling a nobler and a better man. No one can go and do a kind deed to another without feeling the better for it; and may we not say that, every time you really feel nobler and better, your feeling is an indication that you have drawn near to God? This is a fact that we ought to keep in mind when we pray that we may know God's nearness. Some think dimly of a vision. Some . . . half expect to hear a voice. To others God's nearness is limited to feelings they have on Sunday nights in church, and a good many splendid people discredit their experiences of God because, as they say, 'I never see anything. I never hear a voice. I never feel particularly uplifted in a service.' But surely part of the answer is that whenever thought has its horizons widened and its object directed from self to another; whenever feeling is not just emotion, but a deep passion for the well-being of others; whenever will is strengthened, not in the direction of success for oneself, but of service for others, then just because thought, feeling, and will, the three parts of the self, have all been enlarged, is not this an absolute proof that God Himself has drawn near to us, though He may have drawn near at such a depth that we cannot distinguish completely between Himself and ourselves?

—Leslie D. Weatherhead, *The Transforming Friendship*

86 · REVERENCE FOR LIFE

The ethics of reverence for life makes no distinction between higher and lower, more precious and less precious lives. It has good reasons for this omission. For what are we doing, when we establish hard and fast gradations in value between living organisms, but judging them in relation to ourselves, by whether they seem to stand closer to us or farther from us. This is a wholly subjective standard. How can we know what importance other living organisms have in themselves and in terms of the universe?

In making such distinctions, we are apt to decide that there are forms of life which are worthless and may be stamped out without its mattering at all. This category may include anything from insects to primitive peoples, depending on circumstances.

To the truly ethical man, all life is sacred, including forms of life that from the human point of view may seem to be lower than ours. He makes distinctions only from case to case, and under pressure of necessity, when he is forced to decide which life he will sacrifice in order to preserve other lives. In thus deciding from case to case, he is aware that he is proceeding subjectively and arbitrarily, and that he is accountable for the lives thus sacrificed.

The man who is guided by the ethics of reverence for life stamps out life only from inescapable necessity, never from thoughtlessness. He seizes every occasion to feel the happiness of helping living things and shielding them from suffering and annihilation.

Whenever we harm any form of life, we must be clear about whether it was really necessary to do so. . . .

—Albert Schweitzer, *The Teaching of Reverence for Life*

87 · TO KNOW EACH OTHER

[In this dialogue between the dying W. O. Gant and his wife, Eliza, the pathos of two alienated people who have never lived purposefully is vividly shown.]

"Eliza,"—he said—and at the sound of that unaccustomed word, a name he had spoken only twice in forty years—her white face and her worn brown eyes turned toward him with the quick and startled look of an animal—"Eliza," he said quietly, "you have had a hard life with me, a hard time. I want to tell you that I'm sorry."

And before she could move from her white stillness of shocked surprise, he lifted his great right hand and put it gently down across her own. And for a moment she sat there bolt upright, shaken, frozen, with a look of terror in her eyes, her heart drained of blood, a pale smile trembling uncertainly and foolishly on her lips. Then she tried to withdraw her hand with a clumsy movement, she began to stammer with an air of ludicrous embarrassment, she bridled, saying—

"Aw-w, now, Mr. Gant. Well, now, I reckon,"—and suddenly these few simple words of regret and affection did what all the violence, abuse, drunkenness and injury of forty years had failed to do. She wrenched her hand free like a wounded creature, her face was suddenly contorted by that grotesque and pitiable grimace of sorrow that women have had in moments of grief since the beginning of time, and digging her fist into her closed eye quickly with the pathetic gesture of a child, she lowered her head and wept bitterly:

"It was a hard time, Mr. Gant," she whispered, "a hard time, sure enough. . . . It wasn't all the cursin' and the drinkin' —I got used to that. . . . I reckon I was only an ignorant sort of girl when I met you and I guess," she went on with a pathetic and unconscious humor, "I didn't know what married life was like . . . but I could have stood the rest of it . . . the bad names an' all the things you called me when I was goin' to have another child . . . but it was what you said when Grover died . . . accusin' me of bein' responsible for his death because I took the children to St. Louis to the Fair—" and at the words as if an old and lacerated wound had been reopened raw and bleeding, she wept hoarsely, harshly, bitterly—"that was the worst time that I had—sometimes I prayed to God that I would not wake up—he was a fine boy, Mr. Gant, the best I had—like the write-up in the paper said he had the sense an' judgment of one twice his age . . . an' somehow it had grown a part of me, I expected him to lead the others—when he died it seemed like everything was gone . . .

. . . .

"Well, now, Mr. Gant, that's all over, and the best thing we can do is to forget about it. . . . We've both made our mistakes—we wouldn't be human if we didn't—but now we've got to profit by experience—the worst of all this trouble is all over—you've got to think of getting well now, that's the only thing you've got to do, sir," she said pursing her lips and winking briskly at him—"just set your mind on getting well—that's all you've got to do now, Mr. Gant—and the battle is half won. For half our ills and troubles are all imagination," she said sententiously, "and if you'll just make up your mind now that you're going to get well—why, sir, you'll do it," and she looked at him with a brisk nod. "And we've both got years before us, Mr. Gant—for all we know, the best years of our life are still ahead of us—so we'll both go on and profit by the mistakes of the past and make the most of what time's left," she said. "That's just exactly what we'll do!"

And quietly, kindly, without moving, and with the impassive and limitless regret of a man who knows that there is no return, he answered: "Yes, Eliza. That is what we'll do."

—Thomas Wolfe, *Of Time and the River*

88 · ORGANIZATIONAL RELATIONS

Several years ago, the Negro students of a major university asked the local YMCA to help improve communication among the races on the campus. The YMCA responded by asking several of us who were interested in this work to hold weekend retreats for this purpose. The results were fascinating.

On one such weekend, the author went to a camp retreat with about twenty students, Caucasian, Negro, Oriental, about equal numbers of male and female. As usual, the start was slow, cautious, defensive. But as the time went on, gradually, people opened up. Once the students felt comfortable enough, the issues were raised and sharpened.

". . . What are your Negro stereotypes?" "You are dirty, stupid, fleshy, sexually promiscuous." "Yeh, well you, white boy, are exploitative, arrogant, and emotionally inhibited." And what happened after that exchange? Closeness. People began to talk to each other, to dance together, to explore one another as individuals. As one Negro put it, "I didn't lose my stereotypes of twenty years in one weekend, but once I've said them, they don't seem that important. The cards are on the table and we can look at each other as men, and go on from there."

". . . White liberals are just as bad as bigots, almost. They just accept everything I do instead of rejecting it. I could rape your sister and you wouldn't say a word, because I'm black. We don't want that. Know all the bad things about me too."

". . . It's enough to say you treat us equally. How about getting to know me as a person? Building a relation!"

". . . You Negroes are always using your color to excuse everything. Why don't you get off the dime and do something instead of bellyaching?"

. . . .

There seems no question that this type of intimate contact frees people. The relations among many of the participants continued after the weekend. A small island of prejudice had been somewhat eroded. And it occurred in an organizational setting that supported the experience.

—William C. Schutz, *Joy: Expanding Human Awareness*

89 · A DIFFERENT KIND OF NEIGHBORLINESS

. . . The urban secular man is summoned to a different *kind* of neighborliness than his town-dwelling predecessor practiced. Much like the Samaritan described by Jesus in the story he told in response to the question "Who is my neighbor?," his main responsibility is to do competently what needs to be done to assure his neighbor's health and well-being. The man who fell among thieves was not the next-door neighbor of the Samaritan, but he helped him in an efficient, unsentimental way. He did not form an I-Thou relationship with him but bandaged his wounds and made sure the innkeeper had enough cash to cover his expenses.

Urban anonymity need not be heartless. Village sociability can mask murderous hostility. Loneliness is undoubtedly a serious problem in the city, but it cannot be met by dragooning urban people into relationships which sabotage their privacy and reduce their capacity to live responsibly with increasing numbers of neighbors. The church investigators who shook their heads over the evasiveness of the apartment dwellers had forgotten this. They had come to the city with a village theology and had stumbled upon an essential protective device, the polite refusal to be chummy without which urban existence could not be human. They had overlooked the fact that technopolitan man *must* cultivate and guard his privacy. He must restrict the number of people who have his number or know his name.

The small-town dweller, on the other hand, lives within a restricted web of relationships and senses a larger world he may be missing. Since the people he knows also know one another, he gossips more and yearns to hear gossip. His private life is public and vice versa. While urban man is unplugging his telephone, town man (or his wife) may be listening in on the party line or its modern equivalent, gossiping at the kaffee-klatsch.

Urban man, in contrast, wants to maintain a clear distinction between private and public. Otherwise public life would overwhelm and dehumanize him. His life represents a point touched by dozens of systems and hundreds of people. His capacity to know some of them better necessitates his minimizing the depth of his relationships to many others. Listening to the postman gossip becomes for urban man an act of sheer graciousness, since he probably has no interest in the people the postman wants to talk about. Unlike my parents, who suspected all strangers, he tends to be wary not of the functionaries he doesn't know but of those he does.

—Harvey Cox, *The Secular City*

90 · "THE MIRACLE OF DIALOGUE"

We can expect miracles of dialogue because, . . . dialogue brings us face to face with truth in a relationship of love. As each person speaks and responds honestly to the other, each moves toward the other and includes him. This kind of meeting between man and man cannot occur without an implicit meeting between man and God. To really see another is to see the Other, and to really love another is to love the Other. When we are truly known by another we are known by God, and to be truly loved by another is to know the love of God. Dialogue, as we have been thinking of it, is more than communication. It is communion in which we are mutually informed, purified, illumined, and reunited to ourselves, to one another, and God. A spirit pervades and directs the "conversation," and from this spirit, which Christians believe was fully incarnate in Christ, come the fruits of the Spirit. Dialogue is a condition and relationship for the appearance and work of his Spirit, which calls men to, and enables them for, dialogue out of which comes the fruits of dialogue, of the Spirit. —Reuel L. Howe, *The Miracle of Dialogue*

91 · SENSITIVE COMPANIONSHIP

One of the most dedicated participants in the bus protest in Montgomery, Alabama, was an elderly Negro whom we affectionately called Mother Pollard. Although poverty-stricken and uneducated, she was amazingly intelligent and possessed a deep understanding of the meaning of the movement. After having walked for several weeks, she was asked if she were tired. With ungrammatical profundity, she answered, "My feets is tired, but my soul is rested."

On a particular Monday evening, following a tension-packed week which included being arrested and receiving numerous threatening telephone calls, I spoke at a mass meeting. I attempted to convey an overt impression of strength and courage, although I was inwardly depressed and fear-stricken. At the end of the meeting, Mother Pollard came to the front of the church and said, "Come here, son." I immediately went to her and hugged her affectionately. "Something is wrong with you," she said. "You didn't talk strong tonight." Seeking further to disguise my fears, I retorted, "Oh, no, Mother Pollard, nothing is wrong. I am feeling as fine as ever." But her insight was discerning. "Now you can't fool me," she said. "I knows something is wrong. Is it that we ain't doing things to please you? Or is it that the white folks is bothering you?" Before I could respond, she looked directly into my eyes and said, "I don told you we is with you all the way." Then her face became radiant and she said in words of quiet certainty, "But even if we ain't with you, God's gonna take care of you." As she spoke these consoling words, everything in me quivered and quickened with the pulsing tremor of raw energy.

Since that dreary night in 1956, Mother Pollard has passed on to glory and I have known very few quiet days. I have been tortured without and tormented within by the raging fires of tribulation. I have been forced to muster what strength and courage I have to withstand howling winds of pain and jostling storms of adversity. But as the years have unfolded the eloquently simple words of Mother Pollard have come back again and again to give light and peace and guidance to my troubled soul. "God's gonna take care of you."

This faith transforms the whirlwind of despair into a warm and reviving breeze of hope. The words of a motto which a generation ago were commonly found on the wall in the homes of devout persons need to be etched on our hearts:

>Fear knocked at the door.
>Faith answered.
>There was no one there.

—Martin Luther King, Jr., *Strength to Love*

92 · REVOLUTION IN THE LIVES OF THE SAINTS

The secret of the revolution in the lives of the saints lies in the fact that their lives are centered in God. They never seem hurried, they have a large leisure, they trouble little about their influence; they refer the smallest things to God—they live in God. When the revolution in their lives occurs, they seldom leave the church but attempt instead to reform the weaknesses within the church. They rededicate themselves to the betterment of institutions of which they are members. Revolutions without saints usually result in ruthless tyranny and bestial living: this is evidenced in recent revolutions begun by Hitler, Stalin and Mussolini. In our present world, the call is for a spiritual revolution in which Christian saints become leaders.

The saints always seem to have an unassuming heroism, so that they can turn apparent defeat into victory. The Duke of Wellington, in comparing the French and the British soldiers, said, "The British soldiers are not braver than the French soldiers. They are merely braver *five minutes longer.*" The saints are like that. Wherein the ordinary man loses heart, the saint will be braver "five minutes longer." Francis of Assisi wished to become an Umbrian hermit so that he could experience a quiet life of prayer. He was forced instead

to move into preaching, yet he was able to turn an apparent disappointment into a victory which began the Franciscan order of monks. His life, like the lives of other saints, was an "imitation of Christ" and a "practice of the presence of God." Thomas Aquinas once said to Bonaventura, "Show me your library." Bonaventura took Thomas Aquinas to his cell and pointed to a crucifix before which he prayed. "There it is," he said. The courage of the saints issues from the heroism of One who was dauntless until the end.
—Thomas S. Kepler, *A Journey With The Saints*

93 · FOR MY PEOPLE

For my people everywhere singing their slave songs repeatedly: their dirges and their ditties and their blues and jubilees, praying their prayers nightly to an unknown god, bending their knees humbly to an unseen power;

For my people lending their strength to the years, to the gone years and the now years and the maybe years, washing ironing cooking scrubbing sewing mending hoeing plowing digging planting pruning patching dragging along never gaining never reaping never knowing and never understanding;

. . . .

For my people walking blindly spreading joy, losing time being lazy, sleeping when hungry, shouting when burdened, drinking when hopeless, tied and shackled and tangled among ourselves by the unseen creatures who tower over us omnisciently and laugh;

For my people blundering and groping and floundering in the dark of churches and schools and clubs and societies, associations and councils and committees and conventions, distressed and disturbed and deceived and devoured by money-hungry glory-craving leeches, preyed on by facile force of state and fad and novelty, by false prophet and holy believer;

For my people standing staring trying to fashion a better way from confusion, from hypocrisy and misunderstanding, trying to fashion a world that will hold all the people, all the faces, all the adams and eves and their countless generations;

Let a new earth rise. Let another world be born. Let a bloody peace be written in the sky. Let a second generation full of courage issue forth; let a people loving freedom come to growth. Let a beauty full of healing and a strength of final clenching be the pulsing in our spirits and our blood. Let the martial songs be written, let the dirges disappear. Let a race of men now rise and take control.
—Margaret Walker, in *Modern Religious Poems*

CHAPTER 9—TOWARD GREATER DEPTH IN THE EXPERIENCE OF PRAYER

94 · INWARD MUSIC

Prayer, as life, needs its pattern; here too, we can help one another; and here too, the pattern will emerge from the 'priesthood'—from our lively contact with God and our world. In Pasternak's *Dr. Zhivago,* Lara went to church because 'she needed the accompaniment of an inward music, and she could not always compose it for herself.' Liturgy informs prayer. But so does life. Equally needed is the discordant clamour of the secular world. Prayer is the contrapuntal combination of two not entirely dissimilar melodies—God's holiness and God's world.—David Head, *Seek a City Saint*

CHAPTER 9—TOWARD GREATER DEPTH IN THE EXPERIENCE OF PRAYER

95 ·

"I'm going to say my prayers. Anyone want anything?"
—Copyright 1966 Saturday Review, Inc.

96 · THE TRIUMPH OF HIS LOVE

The sacred moments, the moments of miracle, are often the everyday moments, the moments which, if we do not look with more than our eyes or listen with more than our ears, reveal only . . . the gardener, a stranger coming down the road behind us, a meal like any other meal. But if we look with our hearts, if we listen with all of our being and our imagination—if we live our lives not from vacation to vacation, from escape to escape, but from the miracle of one instant of our precious lives to the miracle of the next—what we may see is Jesus himself, what we may hear is the first faint sound of a voice somewhere deep within us saying that there is a purpose in this life, in our lives, whether we can understand it completely or not; and that this purpose follows behind us through all our doubting and being afraid, through all our indifference and boredom, to a moment when suddenly we know for sure that everything does make sense because everything is in the hands of God, one of whose names is forgiveness, another is love. This is what the stories about Jesus' coming back to life mean, because Jesus was the love of God, alive among us, and not all the cruelty and blindness of men could kill him.

—Frederick Buechner, *The Magnificent Defeat*

97 · "DAWN GLISTENS ON THE GRASSES"

We are awake.
Sleep is still in our eyes,
but at once on our lips
shall be your praise.
We glorify, praise, and adore you.
We—that is, the earth,
the water, and the sky;
that is, the grasses and bushes and trees;
that is, the birds and all the other animals;
that is, the people here on earth.
Everything that you have created
enjoys your sun
and your grace
and becomes warm in it.
Dawn glistens on the grasses.
Mist is still hanging in the trees,
and a soft wind
promises a fine day.

CHAPTER 9—TOWARD GREATER DEPTH IN THE EXPERIENCE OF PRAYER

Should we not enjoy everything
that you have created?
We are meant to.
That is why we are so joyful
this dawn,
O Lord.
Grant that the hours and minutes
do not slip away in our hands,
but that we live in your time.
Amen.

—*Prayers by Young Africans,*
I LIE ON MY MAT AND PRAY

98 · OUR NEED TO EXPERIENCE GOD

We can have no idea of what it is like to be God. We wonder if we have very much idea of what it is like to be man.

When we think of You as quite different from ourselves, then we are suddenly aware that You made man in Your likeness. When we speak as though You were a superman, then we are brought up sharply by all that has been said in our day about false and small images of Your true Being. Whether our thinking is done in the odd moments of reflexion, or in a life's work of systematic theology, we despair of our thinking about You. We are no longer sure what our words mean.

What we need is to experience You. But how? We are afraid of turning on our own emotions; we deplore self-deception. We are chary of religious experience, and wary of religious certainty. Yet we experience 'life'. Are we so sure what that is? Every day and every night brings it. Is this, whether we know it or not, our experience of You?

—David Head, *Seek A City Saint*

99 · MIDNIGHT MEDITATION

Almighty God, I have asked Thy help these many times, but it does not come quickly. So often I am depressed and in despair, and I am ashamed to think how easily the tears flow. Since my wife died, I have discovered that I am an old man, with little to light my path. They have been good to me here. Best of all have been the times when I have made a friend of a fellow voluntary patient, and we have walked the green lanes together. But they come and go. I have nothing to go to. I hate to walk alone.

I have been a Churchman all my life, and in my humble way have tried to live up to it. I have been kind and meek by nature, and glad to be so. Now this thing has swept me off my feet, has turned me in upon myself, has gone over my head like a flood, and left me without heart and without hope. I cry to Thee. Canst Thou hear my feeble and desperate moan?

. . . .

This afternoon the chaplain came. We do not see him often. He has far too many to visit. He came today, and he could see I wanted to talk. We stood in the hall of the villa, away from the noise of the radio and the TV, and he talked of Thee.

He didn't invite me to the Sunday Service, and he didn't tell me to pray more, and he didn't tell me I needed more guts (as a clergyman did once), and he didn't tell me to snap out of myself. In a way, he disappointed me. I did not get what I expected and thought I needed. He told me to think about Jesus Christ, and to see Thee in Him. He told me Thou art a God of health and peace, and that Thou art all the time busy to make men whole.

He told me to turn my thoughts away from these weighty burdens toward Thee. He told me to sit for minutes together, as relaxed as I possibly could be, saying over and over, "I am the Lord who loveth and healeth thee." He said that Thou canst not work without faith, and that faith is not making a desperate effort to believe something, but turning to Thee in mind and heart again and again.

So I have been trying, and now—lying in bed—this is the longest prayer I've prayed since I was admitted. My mind keeps coming back to myself, and how things have worked out, and how I had to come to this place, and how alone I am, and how little the future has for me. If only we'd had children. If only I'd been more patient with my wife in those last years. If only she were still with me at home.

I'm doing it again! "I am the Lord who loveth and healeth thee." —David Head, *Stammerer's Tongue*

100 · THE PRINCIPLE OF ALTERNATION IN PRAYER

. . . Each aspect of life apart from its alternate becomes a mechanism. And the whole of human existence falls into two phases, work and worship; the domain of duty and the domain of love, respectively.

. . . .

Any given moment of life must choose between two goods, psychologically incompatible. On the one hand, the peace of the hermit, the silence of the forest, the exaltation of sacrifice, the mightiness of simplification and unity, the joy of self-abandonment, the calm of absolute contemplation, the vision of God. On the other hand, the variety and stress of life, the zest of common ends, the mastery of means, the glory of infinite enterprise, the pride of creativity and self-possession. The modern world as a whole has made its choice. But there is a better choice: namely, the choice of both. For the life of each is that it may lose itself, from time to time, in the life of the other. And this, which is obvious in things partial, is true—and even chiefly true—in things total.

—William Ernest Hocking
The Meaning of God in Human Experience

101 · "PATHWAYS OF THE INNER LIFE"

... The intimate relationship between the soul and God is not the result of man's efforts but of God's initiative. We would not seek God were we not sought by God. Christian mysticism originates in the secret operation of the Holy Spirit which cleanses, revives, comforts and directs the soul. It follows from this that the attitude of a Christian is an attitude of voluntary submission and obedience to the Spirit. It is sometimes described as passivity; yet passivity somehow implies inertia and the mystic is anything but inert under the divine motion. We would rather think in terms of receptivity, which implies open-mindedness, watchfulness, docility, prompt reactions and readiness to co-operate. These are the marks of the new life.

—*Pathways Of The Inner Life*, (Georges A. Barrios, Ed.)

102 · HUNGER OF SPIRIT

Each of the foods by which our spirit lives makes us hungry for the rest. . . .

—Richard C. Cabot, *What Men Live By*

103 · THE OVERVIEW

It is especially when we are confused and uncertain what next to do that we turn from partial to wider views. When lost in the woods you climb the highest tree in sight. From the top of it you may be able to see where you have come from, where you are, and where you should go next. Such a view is precisely what prayer gives. It orients us. As we look over our stumbling, circuitous past we see where we have vered from the track that we meant to keep. We see just where our mingled success and failure have landed us. We look ahead and shape our course afresh.

It takes time, this tree-climbing, and in any party of woodsmen there is usually one who begrudges that time. . . .

But it is the greenhorn, not the old woodsman, who chafes at the halt for a look around. The best way to get ahead is sometimes to stop short and see where we are. The best way to advance our work is, sometimes, to lay it aside and go to bed. On the whole, all things considered, we may find ourselves on the wrong track. Then our pause has been time well spent. —Richard C. Cabot, *What Men Live By*

104 · SPONTANEOUS PRAYER

. . . In a brief Thanksgiving message taped at a television studio in Philadelphia some years ago, I noted that President Johnson in his Thanksgiving Proclamation asked us to pray for our own men in Vietnam and the South Vietnamese. I said that I wished he had gone on to suggest that we pray as well for the Vietcong and North Vietnamese men. We do have it on good authority that we are to pray for our enemies. After the taping, as I was leaving the studio, a cameraman came up to me and said, "Whaddya mean, pray for the Vietcong. We gotta kill those bastards. In wartime this Christianity stuff has to be put aside so we can get the job done." We talked together for a while, and it developed that the man was a loyal churchman. Only as we pray for enemies, national and personal, can we begin to see them as brothers and not bastards, literally bound to us and we to them by the Spirit in human solidarity, the solidarity of sinners called to be saints. . . .

. . . .

Such prayers-on-location will be brief, direct, immediate, spontaneous, often silent, rising out of the anguish or joy of the moment. When you see the hostile one, "Brother Saul, brother George." When joy takes you by surprise, "Thank you, Lord!" When you see the suffering, deceit, longing, loneliness, hope of another, "God bless you." "Christ, have mercy on Bob, Sue." When under pressure, "Lord, help me," "strengthen me," "forgive me," "deliver me." It is said that Martin Luther, when he became afraid or uncertain, would pray, "I am baptized; I am baptized," reminding himself who he was and whose he was, and that the hand of Christ was irrevocably on him no matter what.

—Robert A. Raines, *The Secular Congregation*

105 · "YOU'RE ON TO US"

[Underprivileged and hurt children and youth in jails and detention homes helped Chaplain Burke translate this ancient prayer into modern language.]

Almighty God, unto whom all hearts are open, all desires known and from whom no secrets are hid: Cleanse the thoughts of our hearts by the inspiration of thy Holy Spirit that we may perfectly love thee and worthily magnify thy Holy Name; Through Christ our Lord.

    God, we can't con you
    You're on to what we think
    So clean us up

Then what we say will be square
And we will live on the level.
May Christ help us to do this.
—Carl F. Burke, *Treat Me Cool, Lord*

106 · FOR MORNING, MIDDAY, AND EVENING

In the Morning

Father, with the waking day, our spirits wake to new gratitude for thine unfailing mercies, and we pray that with new strength we may serve thee in whatever work we shall be called this day to do; through Jesus Christ our Lord. *Amen.*

At Midday

O God, through whose good gifts our bodies are again refreshed, may the lifting up of our thoughts to thee refresh our souls with strength and purpose for the unfinished day. *Amen.*

At Evening

Father, as the day draws to its close, we thank thee for our goings out and our comings in, for work and rest, and for the blessings of home about us as we gather again for the food thy grace has given. Be with us in the evening and through the night, and help us to remember trustfully that the darkness and the light are both alike to thee; through Jesus Christ our Lord. *Amen.*
—Walter Russell Bowie, *Lift Up Your Hearts*

107 · H. B. SHARMAN AND PRAYER

. . . There was a brilliant young professor of electrical engineering in the University of Chicago whose name was H. B. Sharman. Agnostic, almost atheistic, he had no use for God or prayer or religion beyond the devotion to humanistic values. One day he heard almost by accident a minister in the chapel give a dare to the students: "If you claim to be scientific in your approach to life, how can you say there is nothing to Jesus' claims to be 'the way, and the truth, and the life' unless and until you have made the experiment of following him. I dare you to get acquainted with Jesus, his life and teachings, to discover what he said about the nature of God, of man and the universe, and to act upon it. Only then will you know whether or not it is true or false."

The young agnostic professor accepted the challenge and for months immersed his mind in the study of Jesus in the four gospels. As he set Jesus continually before him and committed himself to act on the faith Jesus lived, he began to pray. With prayer came a flood of new life. H. B. Sharman dedicated his time from then on to teaching other students the fine art of meditating on the life and teachings of Jesus. . . .

—Lance Webb, *The Art of Personal Prayer*

108 · "WE IS STILL FRIENDS, LORD"

[Chaplain Burke shares this translation of the Eighty-sixth Psalm as it came from the writings of underprivileged children and youth with whom he worked.]

Put your ear next to me, Lord,
I just want you to hear me and talk to me
'Cause I ain't got much.
Just remember I try to be like you
You are my man
So I ask for your help.
Make me happy when I'm mixed up inside.
We know you don't hold nothing against us

And you listen and hear us when we talk to you
And don't push us away.
So when we got troubles
We can call up you.

Help us remember you is only one
And everybody was made by you
And had sure better know it
And you are the only God.
Show me the right side of the street to walk on
So I can walk with you and even trust you
And not be afraid to say it
'Cause your love is just great.

When it seems like everybody is against me
And nothing goes right
And people is out to get me
Help me to know we is still friends
And that your love is here.
That's what helps me have heart.
So "give me some skin," [shake hands with me] Lord,
Then everybody will know where we stand.
—Carl F. Burke, *Treat Me Cool, Lord*

CHAPTER 10—INNER TRANSFORMATION THROUGH CHRISTIAN FELLOWSHIP

109 · MISTAKEN NOTIONS OF FELLOWSHIP

Several mistakes are current in our thinking concerning the nature of Church fellowship. For one thing, there is a general impression that it can be produced as, let us say, one builds a table. Devices, techniques, "tricks of the trade," are employed in order to bring about fellowship. To be sure there are means of encouraging fellowship, . . . Yet there can be no assurance that any of these devices will lead to anything deeper than conviviality. Christian fellowship is something that happens as a result of the operation of the Spirit, and human contrivances may be a hindrance as well as a help in setting the conditions under which the Spirit can become known.

Related to this mistake is a similar one: namely, that fellowship is a distinct and separate phase of the work of the Church. Perhaps it is necessary functionally to have a committee, commission, or program area set up to be concerned with fellowship, but to think of this group as being solely responsible for, or capable of, making the Church into a fellowship is a great mistake. . . .

A third mistake common to our thinking is that fellowship in the Church is on a human level only, and further that the fellowship of the Spirit is an individual fellowship, while fellowship with one another is social. We often forget the statement attributed to Jesus, "Where two or three are gathered in my name, there am I in the midst of them" (Matt. 18:20). . . .

A fourth mistake is the opposite of what has just been stated: whereas Christian fellowship is more than conviviality and while discussion in distinctly religious terms will normally be a part of Christian fellowship, pious words and phrases do not create fellowship. Some of the bitterest feelings arise in the midst of theological discussions! In some circles the two subjects most under taboo are politics and religion. . . .

. . . .

All this adds up to the conclusion that fellowship on a Christian level is something which, like man's salvation, is given to him, yet something which does not become operative until man meets certain conditions. It is significant that Jesus said, "Where two or three are gathered *in my name,* there am I in the midst of them." It should be obvious that being gathered *in the name* of Jesus means being together in his Spirit. —Howard Grimes, *The Church Redemptive*

110 · CHRISTIAN FELLOWSHIP

It should be noted that smallness in and of itself is no guarantee of *koinonia* [KOY-no-NEE-ah; Christian fellowship]. Those groups in which *koinonia* is known are usually doing and sharing quite specific things together. We could take as a norm for the sharing of *koinonia* the practice of the early Christians as described in the second chapter of Acts, especially verse 42: "And they devoted themselves to the apostles' teaching and fellowship, to the breaking of bread and the prayers."

The Apostles' teaching was the witness of those who had known Jesus or heard firsthand stories about Him. It was also the spelling out of the Christian way of life. Some of this teaching has been recorded in the New Testament. Today the Apostles' teaching means Bible study, especially study of the New Testament.

The Apostles' fellowship was a total sharing of life, later described in Acts as including economic sharing. It was a genuine family in Christ.

The breaking of bread was the sharing of Communion, the distinctive Christian act of worship from the very beginning in the early church. Celebrated on Sunday, the day of the resurrection of Christ, this Communion highlighted the presence of the risen Christ as well as re-enacting the death of Jesus, and it looked forward to the communion of the saints in the Kingdom of God.

The prayers included the shared prayer life of fellow believers.

Bible study, sharing of life, Communion, prayer—here are the ingredients which again and again are found to provide the context for *koinonia*. They could almost be described as the conditions for *koinonia*.

The implications of this for the modern church are clear. Conversion takes place in *koinonia*. Therefore, the church must foster and sustain the conditions in which *koinonia* can be known. This cannot be done for most people simply through morning worship. Worship is indispensable as the weekly meeting of the Christian community. But it is effective only as the total sharing of all the people of the friendship in Christ they have known between Sundays. There cannot be real firsthand *koinonia* among hundreds of people. The best evidence of this is the fact that hundreds of people in a given local church can worship faithfully for years without any appreciable change in quality of commitment or direction of life. Many of the same people, exposed to a breath or taste of *koinonia* in some small group, begin to change in a matter of months. The church is obligated to lead its people into small group fellowship where the conditions for *koinonia* prevail. —Robert A. Raines, *New Life in the Church*

111 · HYMNS AND PUBLIC WORSHIP

[Some readers of this satire may consider this reading to be excessive in its emphasis; nevertheless, is it possible to recognize some helpful suggestions for the meaningful singing of hymns?]

. . . The rule for testing a hymn is this: If it emphasizes the attributes of God—His majesty, power, mercy, goodness, love, etc.—or recounts in some manner the story of Jesus, it is an objective hymn and thus, with possible rare exceptions, unsuitable for a public worship service. If on the other hand, the hymn is preoccupied with the feelings, reactions, desires, hopes and longings of the individual worshiper it is subjective and guaranteed to have a religious kick in it.

Illustrations are always more helpful than general rules, so let us consider examples of good and bad hymns.

Some strikes against "A Mighty Fortress"

One hymn which is sung with great frequency in many churches is Luther's "A Mighty Fortress." It is high on the sacred hit parade among seminarians, theologians and the musically educated. This fact alone is enough to make the parish pastor question its acceptability in his congregation, but there are other sound and cogent reasons why it is a bad hymn.

Notice the text. It says:

> A Mighty Fortress is Our God,
> A bulwark never failing;
> Our helper He, amid the flood
> Of mortal ills prevailing:

or this:

> Did we in our own strength confide,
> Our striving would be losing;
> Were not the right man on our side,
> The man of God's own choosing:

. . . .

Picture, if you will, the successful, hard-nosed executives in your congregation arriving at the church in their Cadillacs and Lincolns dressed in Society Brand suits with their wives in mink stoles joining in,

> Others may choose this vain world if they will,
> I will follow Jesus;
> All else forsaking, will cleave to him still,
> I will follow Him

or imagine the president of the local bank chanting,

> Take my silver and my gold,
> Not a mite would I withhold . . .

or a wealthy bachelor with a stable of comely lady friends and a taste for exotic foods and rare wines solemnly intoning,

> Earthly pleasures vainly call me . . .
> Nothing worldly shall enthrall me . . .

or the average collection of Christian saints who know full well that the church is split into denominational segments too numerous to count pooling their enthusiastic voices in,

> We are not divided, all one body we,
> One in hope and doctrine, one in charity.

. . . .

Here is a mystery. How can relatively sane, intelligent people happily sing what amounts to nonsense, or claim, through song, to believe what they obviously do not believe, or promise via hymnody to do what they haven't the faintest inclination to do, and would be stunned if, after the amen, were told to go and do what they just finished saying they were going to do ("Take my silver and my gold, Not a mite would I withhold" for example). As you ponder this paradox your confidence in the author's counsel may be weakened.

—Charles Merrill Smith
How to Become a Bishop Without Being Religious

CHAPTER 10—INNER TRANSFORMATION THROUGH CHRISTIAN FELLOWSHIP

112 ·

If I worship you, Lord, will you give me peace of mind?

... and fame, and success in business?

... and give a personal, written guarantee of immortality for me and my family?

Oh— I must worship you "because you are God"?

What kind of a deal is that?
—Jim Crane, *On Edge*

113 · WORSHIP IN A MISSIONARY CONGREGATION

... In a sanctuary seating about three hundred the pews were taken up in order to make way for long tables across the front half of the church. One hundred and fifty or more people could then gather in the sanctuary for a fellowship meal just as Jesus gathered in the upper room for the Last Supper with his disciples. The meal began about eight o'clock with the congregation sitting at the tables which had been spread with big loaves of Italian bread, jugs of wine, and platters of sardines, symbolic of the connection between the feeding of the five thousand and the elements of the Lord's Supper. During the meal people spontaneously led in the singing of hymns, and there was a general time of fellowship together. Following the meal the minister stood in front of the large communion table which dominated the chancel of the church and preached briefly on the servanthood of the disciples, using as his text the passage from the Last Supper where Jesus insisted on washing his disciples' feet. . . . The minister spoke of the reason why he wore a stole, derived from the Latin word for towel and now a reminder of the towel with which Jesus girded himself and washed the feet of his disciples at the last supper. Following the sermon the minister went to the bottom steps of the chancel. In groups of eight those who had gathered at the tables came and stood facing him on the steps. Kneeling down he wiped the toes of their shoes with a rag which had been sewn into the end of his stole—again a vivid reminder of the nature of his ministry and a re-enactment of the act of Jesus with his disciples. When this foot-washing service had been completed the people brought a loaf of bread and the wine remaining from the meal at the tables and placed it on the communion table as the whole congregation gathered around in three large circles. Then the ordinary bread of the supper was broken and the wine was poured out. The elements were passed from hand to hand as at the Last Supper. When everyone had received the bread they all ate together just as a family might partake together when all had been served. Likewise everyone drank together as a further symbol of their unity. . . .

—George W. Webber, *The Congregation in Mission*

114 · A PRACTICAL STARTING POINT

Unless we have a better study of theology in the Church there will be a disastrous falling away. Many members admit, when pressed, that they think that much of what the leaders of the Church are saying is not true and is said only as a kind of ritual. Thousands, who try to be good Christians, are deeply worried about the contrast between science and religion, convinced that scientific truths are verified, while religious truths are only affirmed. Nearly all of this problem could be solved by a better understanding of the impossibility of absolute proof, in science or anywhere else, and by a deeper conception of what the evidence for the basic Christian affirmation really is. Almost any thoughtful student can come to see that the alleged contrast between scientific certainty and religious wish-thinking is not what it is popularly supposed to be.

The best insurance against falling away is the development of a profound and well-grounded set of convictions. . . .

The purpose of teaching theology is not merely that of the confirmation of the faith of the members, in order to keep them from falling away. It is also preparation for their confrontation with questioning in the world. When a man on the production line is confronted by the doubts of a fellow worker whose wife is dying of cancer, it is not sufficient for him to say "Go to see my pastor." He must be ready to have a convincing answer when it is put, for that is the crucial time. "Always be prepared to make a defense to any one who calls you to account for the hope that is in you, yet do it with gentleness and reverence" (I Peter 3:15). One of the primary tasks of the Christian pastor is to engage in such teaching that the ordinary member, who is his theological student, can be effective when he is faced with the hard questions. Such teaching is never perfectly done, but it can be done in part, and some pastors do it amazingly well.

—Elton Trueblood, *The Incendiary Fellowship*

115 · ONE GROUP TRIED THIS

My proposal is a concession to sin and a compromise with goals, and I acknowledge this at the very outset. But it is proposed as a possibility for local churches to lay hold of. No promises of immediate or even potential success are mentioned. My proposal calls for the institution of contract groups, so-called because of the manner of their formation and from their opening sessions. . . . The contract group is *ad hoc*. It is a terminal group. It *has* a teacher, but the teacher is a book—or a series of books. Its members listen to the teacher through reading and occasionally meet together for the same reasons that they have to go once in a while to the library. The members apply mutual pressure on one another to fulfill their original "contract." When the obligations of the contract are met, the group disbands.

. . . .

The basic contract is a stated normative quality of study demanded—and accepted. The contract mutually agreed on by its members binds them to the performance of intellectual tasks of a publicly stated and a publicly agreed-upon nature. Not only is the content agreed upon but also the style of dealing with the content. The members agree together that they will treat the book (or books) with respect; that they will let its own printed words be the agreed-upon criterion for its own interpretation; that they will not tolerate misrepresentation or misquotation; that they will aim in their study toward the fullest possible comprehension of what they agree to study. Mere verbal assent to these conditioning requirements for contract group membership does not, of course, necessarily mean that the members are going to be conditioned. But public acceptance along with other contracting members concretely represents more than mere verbal assent. . . .

. . . .

The test session becomes a clearinghouse for the ideas in the books. According to the contract, the text itself is the teacher and its own best interpreter, so questions of meaning that arise between members can be resolved only by the text, not by loud shouting or moving for consensus. . . .

The life of the contract group alternates between private reading and public testing at a pace predetermined by the end time, and with a teacher whose intellectual gestures and syntactical aplomb offer to the privileged student a scale of values and a knowledge of the teacher as an educated man. What comes out of such study? A number of people who are informed because they have thought. . . .

—John R. Fry, *A Hard Look at Adult Christian Education*

116 · ALCOHOLICS ANONYMOUS

. . . It is perhaps not farfetched to see an analogy between the workings of Alcoholics Anonymous and those of the early Methodists. I do not for a moment suppose that there has been any conscious imitation of the early Methodists in the methods of Alcoholics Anonymous. But this organization, which has had a more successful record than any I know in looking after alcoholics, has followed a method which is in many ways precisely what the early Methodists did. . . .

Alcoholics Anonymous begins with the requirement that a man confess his inability to cope with his temptation. He has to be willing to say: "I am an alcoholic, and I cannot help myself." He has to come to the point where he believes that there must be help from some power outside himself. The likeness to the requirement of the early Methodist preacher that a man must confess his sins and admit his helplessness is evident.

—Umphrey Lee, *Our Fathers And Us*

117 · STEP INTO A CLASS MEETING

Too few Americans remember a Methodist classmeeting of the old order. There they sat, twelve persons "having the form and seeking the power of godliness"; in the center, on the plain table, the leader's Bible; around it, the circle of chairs, each with its occupant.

Generally the leader pitched the tune for an opening hymn:

"All thanks be to God,
Who scatters abroad,
Throughout every place,
By the least of his servants, his savor of grace:
Who the victory gave,
The praise let him have,
For the work he hath done;
All honor and glory to Jesus alone!"

Followed prayer, fervent, from the heart, that the Spirit of God might be present, to expose the inmost thoughts and

CHAPTER 10—INNER TRANSFORMATION THROUGH CHRISTIAN FELLOWSHIP

imaginings, and to inspire all to new heights of living, and after that the reading of a passage of Scripture, with perhaps a running fire of commentary from the class leader.

"Brother Watson," the leader would demand, the reading done, "how has it been this week with your soul?"

Stammeringly, the lad from the farm just outside the village would rise to his feet. Words would not seem to come. At last, with a mighty wrench, "I thank the Lord, well," he would mumble, and sit down.

But the old leader was not satisfied.

"Praise the Lord," he would encourage, and then the probe would go in. "No wrestlings with temptation?"

"Yes." The lad's head might hang, but there was never any thought of holding back an answer.

"Did that old temper rise up again?"

"Yes."

"And did you win the victory?"

"Yes, thank God."

"Hallelujah, Brother Watson. Go on as you are and one day the crown incorruptible will certainly be yours.

'I the chief of sinners am,
But Jesus died for me.' "

And the circle would take up and carry to its end the familiar stanza. The next chair would bring a very different type of problem.

"Sister Lee, has the Lord been your support this week?"

No hesitation now. In a moment Sister Lee is on her feet, pouring out a record of spiritual blessings in rich profusion, the whole interlarded with ejaculations of rapture that stir the little company to increasingly fervent responses.

"The blessing of God is upon me," the rapt woman concludes. "He is my constant portion by day and by night. By him I have been kept all this week from temptation. Life has become a song and a way of glory! Praise his name!"

. . . .

So the conversation passes around the circle. . . .

. . . .

We have spoken thus at length of the class meeting because it was the most important feature of the early Methodist movement. Societies there were, and these later became the individual churches. But the societies were held together, and made vital, by the class meetings.

How many have been the revivals that have stirred men, but that have evaporated without leaving long-surviving trace! That it was not so with the work of the Wesleys was largely because, after men had been moved, after they had come together in societies, John Wesley was not content to lose them in the anonymity that soon descends upon individual members of a great body, but, by the provision of these little classes, with their weekly review, secured a constant guard against sin and indifference among his followers.

—Halford E. Luccock, Paul Hutchinson, and Robert W. Goodloe, *The Story of Methodism*

CHAPTER 11—INNER VICTORIES OF THE SPIRIT

118 · "BUT GOD'S OWN DESCENT"

But God's own descent
Into flesh was meant
As a demonstration
That the supreme merit
Lay in risking spirit
In substantiation.
Spirit enters flesh
And for all it's worth
Charges into earth

In birth after birth
Ever fresh and fresh.
We may take the view
That its derring-do
Thought of in the large
Is one mighty charge
On our human part
Of the soul's ethereal
Into the material.
—Robert Frost, *In The Clearing*

119 · TOO MUCH MEANING?

Man's problem is not that he is naturally strengthless and finds no meaning in life, but on the contrary that he is too strong, too able, finds too much meaning on interesting side journeys. "Sin" does not consist in worthlessness and depravity, but in idolatrous, wrongheaded worthwhileness and dexterity. Man's predicament does not consist in helplessness, but of being diverted from his active pilgrimage toward fulfillment by the immensely tempting small, limited areas of life which surround him. Saving grace is not "strength" of some kind, for we already have plenty of that, both physical and moral; grace is direction, a sense of time and terrain, a comprehension of value, the gift of moving into the presence of God and the others, and of moving with the others toward the future. —James Sellers, *Theological Ethics*

120 · THE WILL TO WIN

The true believer draws from his faith the strength to persevere despite every obstacle. I am reminded of a young woman who had been obliged by serious functional digestive troubles to abandon all activity and give up her career. The slightest effort caused such a painful recurrence of the trouble that she was compelled immediately to desist. I followed her progress over a number of years. Every form of medical and psychological treatment that I tried failed to give relief: the pains persisted. I was often near despair. But at such moments, when I was ashamed at feeling myself so useless to her, it was she who restored my courage. She would always reply: 'I believe that God has a purpose for me, and that you can help me to find it.'

One day she told me of a vocation she had received while at prayer—a particular hard and difficult one from the human point of view. First I persuaded the head of an educational establishment, a very understanding woman, to take her on with a part-time curriculum: my patient could work for only a few hours a day, and even that cost her unutterable pain. But, sustained by her conviction, she successfully completed this stage in her progress. Now she must envisage a course of study as an internal student. How would she be able to endure the dietary régime imposed on all the students? How could she work regularly enough to pass her examinations?

Of course it required God's help, and the perseverence that comes with faith. The pains still persisted, but the patient would not let anything stop her. It is now two years since she entered upon the career at which she had been aiming. 'Two years of happiness,' she writes to me today, 'in a task given by God and performed without physical hindrance. . . . Since I have been here I have been completely free of my nervous troubles. . . . It is in accomplishing a freely accepted task that a sick person rediscovers the harmony of the body, and hence spiritual harmony.'

—Paul Tournier, *The Strong and The Weak*

121 · EVERYTHING AND EVERYONE AS COMMODITY

... Modern man is alienated from himself, from his fellow men, and from nature. He has been transformed into a commodity, experiences his life forces as an investment which must bring him the maximum profit obtainable under existing market conditions. Human relations are essentially those of alienated automatons, each basing his security on staying close to the herd, and not being different in thought, feeling or action. While everybody tries to be as close as possible to the rest, everybody remains utterly alone, pervaded by the deep sense of insecurity, anxiety and guilt which always results when human separateness cannot be overcome. Our civilization offers many palliatives which help people to be consciously unaware of this aloneness: first of all the strict routine of bureaucratized, mechanical work, which helps people to remain unaware of their most fundamental human desires, of the longing for transcendence and unity. Inasmuch as the routine alone does not succeed in this, man overcomes his unconscious despair by the routine of amusement, the passive consumption of sounds and sights offered by the amusement industry; ...

Man's happiness today consists in "having fun." Having fun lies in the satisfaction of consuming and "taking in" commodities, sights, food, drinks, cigarettes, people, lectures, books, movies—all are consumed, swallowed. The world is one great object for our appetite, a big apple, a big bottle, a big breast; we are the sucklers, the eternally expectant ones, the hopeful ones—and the eternally disappointed ones. Our character is geared to exchange and to receive, to barter and to consume; everything, spiritual as well as material objects, becomes an object of exchange and of consumption.

—Erich Fromm, *The Art of Loving*

122 · THE QUALITY OF WHOLENESS

[In a recent play, Sir Thomas More, highest legal advisor to the throne, refuses to sanction or bless the marriage of Anne to King Henry VIII of England. Henry VIII has divorced Catherine; however, the Church at Rome did not recognize the divorce. Sir Thomas More, loyal to the church and now removed from high office, spends his years in prison. He is brought at last to trial on false charges and condemned to death.]

MORE   Yes. (*He rises; all others sit*) To avoid this I have taken every path my winding wits would find. Now that the Court has determined to condemn me, God knoweth how, I will discharge my mind . . . concerning my indictment and the King's title. The indictment is grounded in an Act of Parliament which is directly repugnant to the Law of God. The King in Parliament cannot bestow the Supremacy of the Church because it is a Spiritual Supremacy! And more to this the immunity of the Church is promised both in Magna Carta and the King's own Coronation Oath!

CROMWELL   Now we plainly see that you *are* malicious!

MORE   Not so, Master Secretary! (*He pauses, and launches, very quietly, ruminatively, into his final stock-taking*) I am the King's true subject, and pray for him and all the realm . . . I do none harm, I say none harm, I think none harm. And if this be not enough to keep a man alive, in good faith I long not to live . . . I have, since I came into prison, been several times in such a case that I thought to die within the hour, and I thank Our Lord I was never sorry for it, but rather sorry when it passed. And therefore, my poor body is at the King's pleasure. Would God my death might do him some good . . . (*With a great flash of*

scorn and anger) Nevertheless, it is not for the Supremacy that you have sought my blood—but because I would not bend to the marirage!
(Immediately the scene change commences, while NORFOLK *reads the sentence)*

NORFOLK   Prisoner at the bar, you have been found guilty on the charge of High Treason. The sentence of the Court is that you shall be taken from this Court to the Tower, thence to the place of execution, and there your head shall be stricken from your body, and may God have mercy on your soul!
—Robert Bolt, *A Man for All Seasons*

123 · COURAGE, FAITH, LOVE

To have faith requires *courage,* the ability to take a risk, the readiness even to accept pain and disappointment. Whoever insists on safety and security as primary conditions of life cannot have faith; whoever shuts himself off in a system of defense, where instance and possession are his means of security, makes himself a prisoner. To be loved, and to love, need courage, the courage to judge certain values as of ultimate concern—and to take the jump and stake everything on these values.

This courage is very different from the courage of which that famous braggart Mussolini spoke when he used the slogan "to live dangerously." His kind of courage is the courage of nihilism. It is rooted in a destructive attitude toward life, in the willingness to throw away life because one is incapable of loving it. The courage of despair is the opposite of the courage of love, just as the faith in power is the opposite of the faith in life.

Is there anything to be practiced about faith and courage? Indeed, faith can be practiced at every moment. It takes faith to bring up a child; it takes faith to fall asleep; it takes faith to begin any work. But we all are accustomed to having this kind of faith. Whoever does not have it suffers from overanxiety about his child, or from insomnia, or from the inability to do any kind of productive work; or he is suspicious, restrained from being close to anybody, or hypochondriacal, or unable to make any long-range plans. To stick to one's judgment about a person even if public opinion or some unforeseen facts seem to invalidate it, to stick to one's convictions even though they are unpopular—all this requires faith and courage. To take the difficulties, setbacks and sorrows of life as a challenge which to overcome makes us stronger, rather than as unjust punishment which should not happen to *us,* requires faith and courage.

The practice of faith and courage begins with the small details of daily life. The first step is to notice where and when one loses faith, to look through the rationalizations which are used to cover up this loss of faith, to recognize where one acts in a cowardly way, and again how one rationalizes it. To recognize how every betrayal of faith weakens one, and how increased weakness leads to new betrayal, and so on, in a vicious circle. Then one will also recognize that *while one is consciously afraid of not being loved, the real, though usually unconscious fear is that of loving.* To love means to commit oneself without guarantee, to give oneself completely in the hope that our love will produce love in the loved person. Love is an act of faith, and whoever is of little faith is also of little love. Can one say more about the practice of faith? Someone else might; if I were a poet or a preacher, I might try. But since I am not either of these, I cannot even try to say more about the practice of faith, but am sure that anyone who is really concerned can learn to have faith as a child learns to walk. —Erich Fromm, *The Art of Loving*

124 · RELIGION IN PRESENT TENSE

What [the Christian] religion says, how it says it, must change and change and change again; but saying Yes to life and its highest values—this is the constant. And this is the reason for the religious institution, all its problems and hazards notwithstanding. Sometimes it is easy to affirm life, and then I want to go someplace with other people and sing out that I am here in this world! I want to see affirmation acted, danced, painted, hear it played and sung. Sometimes life is hard to affirm, and when the blows of circumstance descend on me, I want to go someplace with other people and be reminded by the arts and acts of a community that affirmation is a fact larger than my private sorrow or trouble, that it exists in spite of me at the moment, and that if I can just hang on, I will come here and praise life again—or if not I, then others will. I need to praise the creativity, personal, social, universal, that saves us; praise the knowledge that frees us; praise the love that operates among us—and I need to accept the fact of suffering and death as the price we pay for it all. I need religion to make me rich enough to pay that price and pay it without bitterness.

—Mary Jean Irion, *From the Ashes of Christianity*

125 · CLING TO GOD

. . . One learns . . . . to distinguish between faith and optimism. It is a hard struggle, in which ground is frequently lost as soon as it is gained. Often one is near to despair. But in spite of all our back-sliding the upward march always begins again so long as we go back faithfully each time to ask on our knees for the assistance of God's grace. At last the day comes when we can see the fruits of this unremitting perseverance. Grace has grown. The climate of our lives has gradually changed, in spite of the alternation of defeat and victory. And in this new climate victories are more easily won. Our natural propensity towards disorder, flight, and discouragement are indeed stubborn; but for that very reason we shall, through the months and the years, have multiplied our experiences of liberation. In the end of the day that is what counts: the need to cling always to God, the habit, if I may call it that, of coming back to him, of familiarity with him, which is in a sense imposed on us by the very difficulty of the enterprise.

—Paul Tournier, *The Strong and the Weak*

126 · SAY SOMETHING TO THE WORLD
PART A

The experiences of pain will come to us all. But nothing can ever come to us that may not be captured for God and for the gain of our personal character by an adoption of the right attitude. To one man a set of experiences are great mysteries, baffling problems, heavy burdens. To another those selfsame experiences will be, in Samuel Rutherford's phrase, the kind of burden that "sails are to a ship, that wings are to a bird." . . . To one man, life's experiences are those of dark valleys, steep mountains, rough places. To another every valley becomes exalted, every mountain and hill is brought low, the rough places are made plain, because he has found an attitude which, applied to them, subdues them.

There are still many questions that we cannot answer about pain.

PART B

We cannot understand pain altogether, nor justify it, nor explain it, but we know him [God]. That assurance runs like a silver cord through all the maze of men's experience through all the ages as they are confronted by this mystery. Better men than ourselves have found that just to hold to that cord and trust in the dark is in itself the defeat of pain.

Though there should be every reason in the world to prove that God is a devil; that evil is more powerful than good; that there is no order, no purpose, no living design, no meaning in life at all, yet in the face of all argument to say, "I know," that is to keep alive the undying fire of faith and to make of the very things that would quench it, fuel that shall make it a blazing furnace.

Thus we may not solve the mystery entirely, but we may rise above it, rob it of its power to quell us; more than that, we may turn its fruit of doubt into faith, its depression into victory, its evil into a power for good that none can stay, knowing if "God were one whit less than He is, He dare not put us into a world that carries so many arguments against Him." . . .

—Leslie D. Weatherhead, *Salute to a Sufferer*

127 · LET US BE THANKFUL

. . . Because Christ is our hope, our first and last word should be thankfulness:

Let us be thankful that he has placed us in this time of turmoil and change and called us to be co-workers with him.

Let us be thankful for the new techniques which tend to make life less of a burden for so many men and women and bring relief and new means of living to the less developed parts of the earth.

Let us be thankful that the present means of communication force us to think of mankind as a whole, so that where one member suffers, all suffer.

Let us be thankful that so many new nations have achieved at least a minimum of freedom and that others are on the way to it.

Let us be thankful for the growing thirst for human justice that one finds today in so many parts of the world.

Let us be thankful that the young generation rejects the *status quo* of easy conformity and wants to move ahead, even if it means some blundering.

Let us be thankful for every genuine search for truth, for the scientist and the artist and every worker who does his job honestly.

Let us be thankful for the signs of renewal in the various Christian confessions, for all courageous witness and every humble sign of love.

Let us be thankful for the ecumenical movement, for all joint efforts in prayer, witness, and practical service.

Let us be thankful because Christ, our hope, is stirring his church and his world to ever-new faith and action.

Let us be thankful, above all, because he, Christ, is the Lord of our life and of all life.

—Suzanne de Dietrich, *God's Word in Today's World*